GLOBETROTTER™

Travel

D0795164

ISRAEL

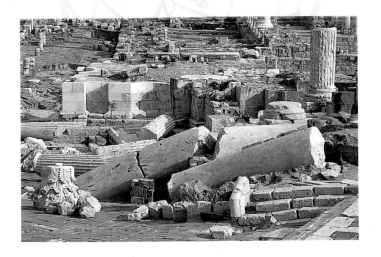

Sue Bryant

NEW
HOLLAND

NEW
HOLLAND

★★★ Highly recommended
★★ Recommended
★ See if you can

Seventh edition published in 2015
by MapStudio™
10 9 8 7 6 5 4 3 2 1
www.globetrottertravelguides.com

Distributed in Africa by
MapStudio™
Unit3, Block B, M5 Park, Eastman Road,
Maitland 7405, Cape Town, South Africa
PO Box 193, Maitland 7404

Distributed in the UK/Europe/Asia by
John Beaufoy Publishing Ltd

Distributed in the USA by
National Book Network

ISBN 978 1 77026 663 6

This guidebook has been written by independent authors and
updaters. The information therein represents their impartial
opinion, and neither they nor the publishers accept payment
in return for including in the book or writing more favourable
reviews of any of the establishments. Whilst every effort has
been made to ensure that this guidebook is as accurate and
up to date as possible, please be aware that the facts quoted
are subject to change, particularly the price of food, transport
and accommodation. The Publisher accepts no responsibility
or liability for any loss, injury or inconvenience incurred by
readers or travellers using this guide.

Commissioning Editor: Elaine Fick
DTP Cartographic Manager: Genené Hart
Editors: Elaine Fick, Thea Grobbelaar, Tarryn Berry,
Susannah Coucher, Catherine Mallinick
Picture Researchers: Shavonne Govender, Colleen
Abrahams, Rowena Curtis
Design and DTP: Nicole Bannister, Lellyn Creamer, Simon
Lewis, Éloïse Moss
Cartographers: Elaine Fick, Reneé Spocter, Genené Hart,
Nicole Bannister
Updated in 2015 by: Mariëlle Renssen
We would like to thank Rabbi Stuart Serwator for his
valuable input.

Reproduction by Hirt & Carter (Pty) Ltd, Cape Town
Printed and bound by Craft Print International Ltd, Singapore

Keep us current
Information in travel guides is apt to change, which is why
we regularly update our guides. We'd be grateful to receive
feedback if you've noted something we should include in
our updates. If you have new information, please share
it with us by writing to the Commissioning Editor at the
MapStudio address on this page. The most significant
contribution to each new edition will receive a free copy of
the updated guide.

Front Cover: *Western Wall and the Dome of the Rock in the
background, Jerusalem.*
Title Page: *The Roman settlement of Tel Beit She'an is being
painstakingly excavated.*

CONTENTS

1
Introducing
Israel

Few sights can be as stirring as **Jerusalem's** golden Dome of the Rock glowing in the sunset, the whole of the honey-coloured city stretched out below, with wild thyme and rosemary scenting the balmy air. But Israel, a tiny strip of land clinging to the edge of the Arabian peninsula, is full of such magnificent views and unexpected contrasts.

There are the bright lights and skyscrapers of lively **Tel Aviv**; or the dazzling salt islands floating on the **Dead Sea**, shimmering in a permanent heat haze. At the northern end of the country are the lush, forested slopes of snowcapped **Mount Hermon** and the foaming rapids of the **River Jordan**, while the south promises the luxurious pleasures of **Eilat**, a thriving holiday resort on the Red Sea, on the edge of the baking **Negev Desert**.

History unravels before you in the Holy Land. Follow the pilgrims along the **Via Dolorosa** in Jerusalem's **Old City**; learn the tragic story of **Masada**, high above the **Dead Sea**; or marvel at the Dead Sea Scrolls, the oldest document known to man, in the **Israel Museum**.

Just over eight million people from five continents have made their home here, each retaining their cultural identity, creating a colourful melting pot with a single goal, to reside and worship in the biblical land of milk and honey. Visitors flock here in their thousands, many of them on the pilgrimage of a lifetime. But even the least religiously inclined cannot fail to be moved by the magnificent landscapes, incredible history and radiant colours of this fascinating country.

TOP ATTRACTIONS

*** **Jerusalem's Old City:** thousands of years of history.
*** **Jaffa Port:** wonderful nightlife and restaurants.
*** **Masada:** 2000-year-old ruins, with a tragic story.
*** **Dead Sea:** float on the mineral-rich sea.
*** **Nazareth:** walk in the footsteps of Jesus.
*** **Sea of Galilee:** green countryside, adventure sports.
** **Akko:** explore the eerie underground Crusader city.
** **Eilat:** indulge in beach life and superb diving.

◄ *Opposite: Traditional Bar Mitzvah celebrations at Jerusalem's Western Wall.*

INTRODUCING ISRAEL

Independence day:
14 May 1948
Members of parliament: 120
Population: 8.146 million
Religion: 80% Jews; the remaining 20% Muslims, Samaritans, Christians, Druze, Baha'i and others
Languages: Hebrew and Arabic. Also spoken: English, French, German, Yiddish, Russian, Spanish, Polish and Hungarian
Highest point: On Mount Hermon massif, 2224m (7296ft)
Lowest point: Dead Sea, about −400m (−1300ft)

▶ *Right: Turbulent on some stretches, tranquil on others, the River Jordan links the Sea of Galilee with the Dead Sea.*

Most of Israel's water for drinking and irrigation comes from the Sea of Galilee. With thousands of tourists a year, salt springs, peat flows and sewage from the area to contend with, the lake's ecosystem is increasingly fragile. The water is dangerously close to its 'red line', the line below which its pollutants become too concentrated for consumption. Israelis are used to conserving water and visitors should respect the notices in hotels asking them to do the same.

THE LAND

Israel is a country of incredible natural diversity. Snow-capped mountains, arid desert, green vineyards and rocky hills all fall within its compact boundaries. The country is just 418km (260 miles) from north to south and 112km (70 miles) at its widest point. Physical borders are formed by the **Mediterranean Sea** to the west, the northernmost fragments of the **Great Rift Valley** to the east, and a narrow finger of the **Red Sea** in the south. Israel shares its political borders with Lebanon, Syria, Jordan, Egypt and the Palestinian Territories.

Mountains and Rivers

The snowcapped **Mount Hermon** massif in the **Golan Heights** carries the country's highest point, at 2236m (7336ft). A lower, undulating range forming the Hills of Galilee, Samaria and Judea forms the spine of the northern end of the country. In the deep south, across the scrub-covered landscape of the **Negev Desert**, the steep hills of the Egyptian Sinai, Jordan and Saudi Arabia plunge into the Red Sea. The Negev itself, meanwhile, has an unusual geology of ancient craters, the best known of which is **Makhtesh Ramon** situated in the town of Mitzpe Ramon, where interesting prehistoric remains have been found. The **Jordan River**, which links the Sea of Galilee – in reality an inland lake – with the Dead Sea, forms the lifeblood of Israel. Fed by three tributaries, **Nahal Hermon**, a spring at the base of Mount Hermon, **Nahal Dan** and **Nahal Senir** from the Lebanon, the river gushes into the Sea of Galilee from the north.

Seas and Shores

The **Dead Sea**, the lowest point on earth at about 400m (1300ft) below sea level, is effectively the end of the Jordan River. Intense heat at this depth causes rapid evaporation, leaving a mineral-rich soup that sustains no life. West of the central hills, the land flattens out into a fertile coastal plain, sloping gently towards the Mediterranean as well as sustaining two large cities, Tel Aviv and Haifa. The plain supports intensive agriculture. The northern end of the Mediterranean coast is a series of scenic rocky peninsulas, hidden bays and coastal mountains, purple in the heat haze. South of Caesarea, however, the shoreline flattens out into one long, straight stretch of sand that continues all the way to the Palestinian Gaza Strip in the far coastal south.

Israel has another, tiny section of shoreline in its deep south, the highly developed resort of **Eilat**, nestling at the tip of the **Red Sea**. Eilat's beaches are carefully protected, as stunning coral reefs lie immediately offshore, just feet below the surface. This, combined with spectacular underwater life, is the reason for the popularity of the Red Sea and nearby Sinai as a diving location.

HEAVENLY HOT MINERAL SPRINGS

Because of its location along a major geological fault line, Israel has various hot mineral springs. One of the best known is at Tiberias on the Sea of Galilee. There are two at the Dead Sea, Zohar and Ein Gedi, and one near Ashkelon in the west, where a series of shallow, mineral-rich pools are located in the grounds of the Kibbutz Sde Yoav. Arad, 620m (2034ft) above sea level, is cool, dry and pollen-free by comparison and serves as a health resort for people suffering from asthma and other respiratory diseases.

▼ *Below: The rocky Negev Desert covers the southern half of the country.*

INTRODUCING ISRAEL

PLANT A TREE FOR ISRAEL

Israelis plant trees for birthdays and weddings. Six million trees have been planted some 20km (12 miles) from Jerusalem in honour of the Jews who died in the Holocaust. For visitors, the Holy Land Foundation coordinates tree planting in six areas of Israel. For a nominal fee, you may plant a tree and receive a certificate, a copy of the *Planter's Prayer* and a lapel pin.

Climate

Summer in Israel extends all the way from April to October, with short, mild winters from November to March. Tel Aviv and Haifa, being coastal cities, are much cooler in **summer** than inland cities, and have an average daily maximum of 30°C (86°F) in August and September, the hottest months, whilst Eilat swelters at 40°C (104°F). The coast and the Jordan River Valley are very humid.

In the north, **winters** are cool with January temperatures dropping to around 6°C (42°F) in Jerusalem and sometimes lower, causing ground frost. Mount Hermon in the Golan Heights is actually a ski resort, while at the same time visitors to the Dead Sea can enjoy daytime highs of 22°C (72°F) in February. Rainfall is low here, even in winter, and the spring showers that feed the Jordan River are vital to the country's water supply.

Plant Life and Wildlife

Thanks to its incredibly diverse landscape, Israel supports an astonishing variety of animals and plants. This was not always the case; under the rule of the Ottoman Turks, mass deforestation meant the land became a dust bowl and many

▶ Right: Israel has many species of tree, some native to the country.

birds and mammals became extinct. The Jewish National Fund has set up a huge reforestation programme (this was started in the 1950s) which has resulted in 10% of the country's land area being covered with trees. In addition, the **Hai-Bar programme** aims to bring back biblical creatures such as the **Addax antelope**, the wild **Asiatic ass** (once ridden by Jesus), the **Mesopotamian fallow deer**, the exquisite **white oryx**

(the creature which spawned the myth of the unicorn) and even **ostrich** to the land of the Bible. This means that more and more rare wild animals are being released in Israel's 280 nature reserves. Elsewhere, mainly deep in the desert or mountains, **gazelle** and **ibex** thrive, as do foxes, wolves and, around Mount Hermon, otters.

▲ *Above: Camels are a regular means of transport for Bedouin people.*

Beautiful forests of **Eurasian oak**, **African acacia** and the native **Jerusalem pine** now cover Israel's soil, with oleander, myrtle and fragrant wild herbs flourishing in the drier areas. Cultivated trees include apricot, almond, citrus and walnut, while more unexpected country scenes include alpine meadows on the slopes of Mount Hermon and the world's northernmost papyrus swamp at nearby Hula. As far back as the 11th century, 'biblical' flowers were prized as souvenirs and many have become extinct, but the beautiful **Madonna lily** (an alpine meadow species) can still be found.

Bird Life

Hundreds of species of migratory birds pass Israel en route from Europe to Africa, among them storks, herons, ducks, pelicans, hawks, gulls, waders, plovers, sandpipers, flamingos and song birds. Once every seven years, when the vineyards are left fallow according to Jewish law, the birds enjoy a free bonanza of ripe grapes. The best place to view these migrants is at **Eilat** in the far south, considered by ornithologists to be among the Mediterranean region's finest spots for bird-watching.

BIRD-WATCHING CALENDAR

Sep—Oct is the best time for observing the migration of predatory birds, storks and pelicans in the Hula Valley. Waterfowl are abundant from Nov—Feb, while the migratory birds return to the north in Mar—Apr. Malagan Michael Nature Reserve is open from Nov—Mar for observation of waterfowl, while Feb—May and Aug—Oct are the best times to enjoy the spectacular migration over Eilat. The North Beach and the salt ponds are a bird-watcher's dream, and viewing times are best in the early morning or late afternoon.

INTRODUCING ISRAEL

HISTORICAL CALENDAR

12,000BC Cave-dwellers in Carmel.

7500BC Settlement in Jericho.

3200BC Canaanite tribes establish fortified cities.

2200–1500BC Abraham founds Hebrew race, Canaan.

1550–1200BC Exodus from Egypt. Delivery of Ten Commandments (Mount Sinai).

1000BC Jerusalem becomes capital of 12 tribes of Israel.

960BC King Solomon builds First Temple.

722BC Northern Kingdom falls to Assyrians; Israelis exiled.

586BC Babylonians destroy the Temple.

535–515BC Temple rebuilt.

332–37BC Hellenistic Period.

166–160BC Desecration of the Temple.

63–4 Herod's rule. Refurbishment of the Temple.

AD20–33 Ministry and crucifixion of Jesus of Nazareth.

AD70 Destruction of Jerusalem by Romans.

AD73 Fall of Masada.

4th Century Christianity official religion of Roman Empire.

622 Birth of Islam; Muslim Arabs conquer Middle East.

637 Jerusalem taken by Arabs.

691 Dome of the Rock built.

1099–1291 Crusader Period; Jews massacred.

1291–1516 Mameluk rule.

1517–1917 Ottoman rule.

1860 First neighbourhoods built outside Old City.

1882 First wave of immigrants (aliya), from Russia.

1889 Opening of Suez Canal revives trade routes.

1897 First Zionist World Congress.

1909 City of Tel Aviv founded outside walls of Jaffa.

1914–18 World War I. Britain promises Palestinian Jews and Arabs liberation.

1917–48 British Mandate. Jewish immigration to Palestine restricted. Six million Jews murdered by the Nazis in World War II.

1948 State of Israel proclaimed. Immediate invasion by Arab armies. Israel divided.

1967 The Six Day War; Jerusalem reunited.

1973 Yom Kippur War.

1978 Egypt and Israel sign Camp David Accord.

1985 Israeli Defence Forces withdraw from Lebanon.

1987 Intifada, the Palestinian uprising. Terrorist attacks.

1990–91 Gulf War; PLO backs Iraq. Tel Aviv bombed.

1993 Peace agreement signed between Rabin and Arafat. Jericho and Gaza Strip under Palestinian self-government.

1994 Land border with Jordan opens at Eilat.

1995 Rabin assassinated.

1999 Likud Party elected.

2000 Second Intifada.

2001 Sharon prime minister.

2002 Israel launches Operation Defensive Shield and builds 'anti-terrorist' fence, cutting off Palestinian areas.

2004 Death of Yasser Arafat.

2005 Israeli settlers withdraw from Gaza.

Jul–Aug 2006 Second Lebanon War.

2007 Renewed Israeli military action in Gaza leads to more violence.

2008 Israel launches Operation Cast Lead in Gaza Strip in response to rocket attacks on southern Israel.

2009 Binyamin Netanyahu elected prime minister.

2010–2014 Uneasy peace reigns as Israeli settlement construction continues on West Bank.

2014 Ongoing US efforts to broker peace negotiations between Israel and Palestinians.

HISTORY IN BRIEF

Situated at the crossroad of two continents, Africa and Asia, and passed by all the great trade routes of the ancient world, it was inevitable that the tiny sliver of land now called Israel should play a dramatic role in world history. Its physical location, combined with the beliefs of three great religions – Christianity, Judaism and Islam – in its spiritual importance, have inspired a ceaseless struggle over the land of milk and honey.

▶ *Opposite: Stunning frescoes can be seen inside Jerusalem's Tower of David. The tower contains the Museum of the History of Jerusalem, detailing aspects of the story of one of the world's most contested cities.*

In the Beginning

Evidence of cave dwellers around **Carmel** has been dated back to 600,000 years before Christ. **Jericho**, one of the oldest cities in the world, was settled about 7000BC, while archaeologists have discovered that **Be'er Sheva** was inhabited in 3200BC. People lived in small villages where they grew crops, farmed animals, made simple tools from copper and bronze and followed pagan religious beliefs.

The Land of Canaan

By 3000BC, Canaanite tribes had established fortified cities in this land

which bordered the two great powers of the time, **Egypt** and **Assyria**, both of whom indulged in frequent, vicious battles along the Mediterranean trade route. New tribes began to arrive; belonging to one of them was the patriarch **Abraham**, believed to have come from Ur in what is now Iraq and to have fathered the Israeli people. Although the only record of Abraham and his sons **Isaac** and **Jacob** is in the Bible, there was certainly a leader of the Israelite tribe who, unlike the other tribes of the time, worshipped a single deity.

By the 13th century BC, Egypt had been weakened in the north by its war with the **Hittite Empire**, a feature of North Syria and Asia Minor during the second millennium BC, and gradually new, smaller powers including Abraham's descendants, the **Israelites**, began to emerge.

The Israelites and the Promised Land

According to the Bible, Abraham's descendants were taken into slavery in Egypt around 1550BC. The **Book of Exodus** tells how they escaped under the leadership of **Moses**, made a miraculous 40-year journey across the wilderness and the Red Sea, and received the **Ten Commandments** on **Mount Sinai** before conquering their Promised Land.

THE BOOK OF EXODUS

The *Book of Exodus* is one of history's great adventure stories. It tells the story of God choosing Moses to lead the 'Children of Israel' out of slavery in Egypt. Ten plagues are inflicted on the Egyptians and the waters of the Red Sea part to allow the fleeing Israelites to cross. Subsequently, in Sinai, while the Israelites are wandering in the wilderness, Moses encounters the burning bush. God then gives Moses the Ten Commandments and the Israelites build the Tabernacle on Mount Sinai into which are placed various sacred furnishings, among them the **Ark of the Covenant**. The Jewish feast of **Sukkot** today recreates the conditions of the wilderness as families eat under temporary shelters outside their homes.

INTRODUCING ISRAEL

The **Israelites** settled in what is now Israel during the early Iron Age (1200BC) and formed a monarchy, headed by **King Saul** whose adopted son and successor, David, led them to final victory over the Philistines, an aggressive race still controlling the coast. Saul himself secured many military victories but it was David who conquered **Jerusalem**, proclaiming it the capital of the 12 tribes of Israel. His son, Solomon, built the First Temple, installing the **Ark of the Covenant** (which contains the two tablets of stone on which were carved the Ten Commandments) to be the focal point for Jewish worship.

By the time of **King Solomon** (950BC), Israel was a powerful land, stretching from the **Red Sea** to the **Euphrates River** in the north. But jealousies between tribes led to 10 in the north forming the **Kingdom of Israel**, while the tribes of Judah and Benjamin formed the southern Kingdom of Judea. Alliances with neighbours continued to be formed and broken until the northern kingdom fell in 722BC to invading Assyria.

Babylonian and Persian Rule

The Israelites from the north were exiled overseas and gradually became absorbed into other societies. The south held out for a further 150 years until the **Babylonians**, who had replaced the Assyrians in power, invaded in 586BC. The Babylonian army crushed Judah, and destroyed the Temple

▶ Right: The original scrolls of the Torah were housed in the Ark of the Covenant, which was kept in the First Temple.

of Jerusalem. The surviving population was exiled to Babylonia, where they mourned for their lost land.

As foretold by the prophets of the time, the Babylonian Empire fell to **Persians** 40 years later and the exiles were allowed to return. The Temple of Jerusalem was rebuilt but tension ran high between the **Jews** (from Judah) and the **Samaritans**, those northerners who had stayed in Israel and married foreign immigrants brought in by the Assyrians.

Roman Times

Alexander the Great defeated the **Persians** in 333BC and for 900 years, Israel was part of the **Greco-Roman Empire**. Hellenic rulers attempted to outlaw Judaism in the 2nd century BC, defiling the Temple in the process. Jewish sovereignty was then re-established, but lasted only until 63BC, when the country was annexed by the **Romans**. **Jesus** was born – and died – at a time when Jews were split into different factions: the wealthy **Sadducees**; the **Pharisees**; the **Essenes**; and fanatical **Zealots**.

United by a hatred for the Romans, the Jews revolted in AD66, only to be crushed three years later. The Temple was destroyed and the final Jewish Zealot stronghold, **Masada**, fell in AD73 with the mass suicide of its inhabitants. The Jewish population that remained around Galilee rebelled again in AD132 but was broken once and for all by the Romans' sheer numbers. Villages were destroyed and many Jews were sold into slavery.

Diaspora

The Jews scattered far and wide, from Egypt to Eastern Europe, where they worked as traders. This became known as the **Diaspora**, the Greek word for 'dispersion'. As **Christianity** became the official religion of the Roman Empire, widespread hostilities against Jews began again, although a community in Babylon, away from the Christian areas, continued to thrive.

In the 7th century the Muslim religion, **Islam**, was founded by the prophet Mohammed. After receiving his first revelation in

THE JEWISH DIASPORA

The Jewish Diaspora, or scattering, began in 587BC, when the kingdom of Judea was conquered by the Babylonians, who destroyed the Temple in Jerusalem and exiled the Jews. When it was rebuilt and the Jews allowed to return, many remained in Babylon. The destruction of the Second Temple by the Romans in BC70 and the second expulsion caused the Jewish population to spread throughout the Roman Empire. In the Middle Ages, fleeing persecution, many settled in Eastern Europe, and in the 20th century, in the Americas. To this day, Jews have remained scattered worldwide; of the 14.5 million in the world, only 6.1 million live in Israel, although all have the right to return. About 6.2 million Jews live in North America, and 1.5 million in Europe. France has the third-largest Jewish population in the world and there are sizeable communities in South Africa and Australia.

INTRODUCING ISRAEL

▲ Above: An early mosaic map representing part of Palestine.

AD616, Mohammed taught in Mecca, his teachings forming the basis of the Qur'an, Islam's sacred scripture. He was forced to flee to Medina in 622, but returned with his followers to conquer Mecca in 630, becoming the recognized prophet of Arabia. Fuelled by this new religion, an Arab invasion took place in AD640, their army storming across what was then Palestine and conquering it. Palestine became part of Syria and Jerusalem was declared a Holy City by the Muslims. The great mosque, the **Dome of the Rock**, was built in 691.

Crusades

Christians in Europe viewed the Arab rule of the Holy Land as an insult, and in the 11th century the **Pope** ordered a series of Crusades, which by 1099 had effectively reconquered Jerusalem, though thousands of Muslims and Jews were slaughtered in the process. After the **Second Crusade** (1147–49) Jews were allowed back into Jerusalem, but the **Third** and **Fourth Crusades**, ending in 1204, were particularly vicious and anti-Semitic, branding Jews as 'God-killers'.

In 1187 **Saladin**, the ruler of Egypt, managed to rout the Crusaders at the Horns of Hittim and Jews were once again allowed to live in Jerusalem. A series of disastrous campaigns was carried out by the Crusaders in an attempt to recoup their losses but in 1291 the Crusader kingdom finally came to an end with the fall of **Akko**, when the Crusaders were defeated by the Muslim Mamelukes who had succeeded Saladin as rulers of Egypt.

The region did not prosper under the Mamelukes, who ruled from 1291 to 1516. The port of Jaffa was largely destroyed for fear of further invasion and the Holy Land became a backwater. Jerusalem was mainly abandoned and poverty was rife.

THE FATHER OF ZIONISM

Born in May 1860 in Budapest, Theodor Herzl is regarded as the father of Zionism. He studied law in Vienna but ended up following a career as a journalist and playwright. Herzl grew increasingly concerned about the rise of anti-Semitism in Vienna in the 1880s – the initial motivation in Zionism was not to preserve a religion, but simply to protect Jewish people. In 1896 he published The Jewish State, a guide to creating a refuge for Jews. In 1897, he organized the first World Zionist Congress in Basel, Switzerland, and set up a Jewish Colonial Trust. He continued to lobby internationally for a home for the world's Jews until his death in 1904.

Ottoman Conquest

The Ottomans ousted the Mamelukes in 1517 and divided the land into four districts which were ruled from Istanbul and administered from the province of Damascus. An estimated 5000 Jewish families lived in the country at this time, in Jerusalem, Nablus, Hebron, Gaza, Safed and the villages around Galilee – a mix of native Jews and early immigrants from Europe. Once again, though, the decline in power of the Ottoman rulers left the region neglected and impoverished, the forests of Galilee and Carmel decimated, to be replaced by swampland and encroaching deserts.

Birth of Zionism

During the 19th century, everything changed. Missionary activity from overseas opened up the Holy Land and encouraged immigration. Trade began to thrive after the opening of the **Suez Canal** in 1889 and the first road was built from Jaffa to Jerusalem. The population expanded and the first neighbourhoods developed outside the city walls of Jerusalem. By the early 20th century, the port of Jaffa was so overcrowded it needed to expand beyond the walls, and in 1909 the city of **Tel Aviv** was established.

Meanwhile, life continued to be tough for the Jewish exiles. The **pogroms**, or mass persecution, of the Jews in Russia, which caused tens of thousands of Jews to flee yet again – some of them to Palestine – gave rise to a new feeling: **Zionism**. This was the call for the establishment of a Jewish state in Palestine, first dreamed of by Russian-born journalist **Peretz Smolenskin**. The idea was brought together by a Viennese journalist and playwright, **Theodor Herzl** (1860–1904), who lobbied the influential to find a home for the scattered Jewish peo-

> ### THE SCROLLS OF HISTORY
>
> The Scrolls were discovered in 1947 by a Bedouin shepherd, who was looking for a lost goat around the shores of the Dead Sea. In the ruined, mountainous settlement of Qumran, once inhabited by the devout Essene people, the Bedouin threw a stone into a cave and heard the sound of pottery being smashed. Further investigation revealed earthenware jars filled with flaking parchment, dating between 100BC and AD100. Subsequent explorations revealed more scrolls and many fragments of pottery, most of which are now housed in the **Israel Museum**.

▼ Below: For centuries, many Jews lived in crowded ghetto conditions in eastern Europe.

INTRODUCING ISRAEL

▲ *Above: The Yad Vashem Memorial in Jerusalem serves as a stark reminder of the Holocaust.*

ple. He published a document, *The Jewish State*, in 1896 and established the **World Zionist Congress** in 1897.

In 1917, in the famous Balfour Declaration, British foreign minister Arthur Balfour promised that Britain would support the establishment of a 'Jewish national home' in Palestine. In the same year, British forces entered Jerusalem under **General Allenby**, ending 400 years of Ottoman rule.

The State of Israel

In July 1922, the League of Nations entrusted Great Britain with the **Mandate for Palestine**. It was decided, however, that the provisions for setting up a Jewish national home would not apply to the area east of the Jordan River, which accounted for three-quarters of the territory included in the Mandate. This region eventually became the Kingdom of Jordan.

Waves of refugees continued to descend on Palestine, threatened by the appointment of the Nazi **Adolf Hitler** as chancellor of Germany in 1933. There was increasing unrest and uprising by Palestinian Arabs, themselves nervous of the growing Jewish power in Palestine.

The British clamped down on immigration, divided between support of the Jews and their need to maintain economic relations with the Arabs. During World War II (1939–45), six million Jews were exterminated by the Nazis, yet the terrified refugees who tried to immigrate after the **Holocaust** continued to be turned away.

Under Irgun leader Menachem Begin, Jewish citizens of Palestine rose up to form a provisional government, desperate to grant the refugees sanctuary. But refugee boats were still turned away. Three determined Jewish militias set out to force the British out of Palestine, each operating in its own way: the Irgun under Menachem Begin, its splinter group the Lehi under Avraham Stern, and the larger and longer-established Haganah organization which at times co-operated with the British. All used highly successful guerrilla operations, and the British instituted severe reprisals. In one of the best-known incidents, Begin's **Irgun** movement planted bombs in the British head-quarters, the **King David Hotel** in Jerusalem, killing 91 people. In 1947 the **United Nations** voted to partition Palestine into a Jewish and an Arab state. The Arabs were outraged. The independent **State of Israel** was proclaimed on 14 May 1948 by Prime Minister **David Ben-Gurion**.

Almost immediately, though, the celebrations ended as Egypt, Jordan, Syria, Lebanon and Iraq invaded the new country. In the ensuing seven-month **War of Independence**, Israel came out victorious but at the cost of 6000 lives. Negotiations for a settlement took place under the United Nations. The Coastal Plain, Galilee and the entire Negev were kept within Israel's sovereignty, Judea and Samaria (the West Bank) came under Jordanian rule, the Gaza Strip came under Egyptian administration, and the city of Jerusalem was divided, with Jordan controlling the eastern part, including the Old City, and Israel the western sector.

In July 1950, the **Law of Return** was passed by the first **Knesset** (parliament), granting all Jews the right to Israel citizenship. More waves of mass immigration followed, along with extensive funding of the new state from Jews living in the worldwide Diaspora.

The new State of Israel remained a cause of concern to the Arab world, so much so, that Nasser (Egypt's new president) nationalized and assumed control of the Suez Canal which had been developed as a private company in which Britain and France were the majority shareholders. France and Britain took military action in 1956 and in the course of events Israel extended her borders, claiming the Gaza Strip and the Sinai as hers. These territories, however, were relinquished to Egypt in the ceasefire agreement between the European powers.

DESERT TOMBS

Israel's first prime minister, David Ben-Gurion, is buried in modest surroundings, deep in the Negev Desert, alongside his wife, Paula, close to the kibbutz where they spent their later years. Their tomb is in a national park (situated on the edge of an escarpment) where local stone and flora blend harmoniously into the barren wastes of the surrounding desert. The tomb is worth a visit for its superb views alone.

CRUSADER CASTLE

One of the most picturesque of the Crusader castles, Nimrod's Fortress stands like a fairy-tale vision on the slopes of Mount Hermon near the Golan Heights, in the north of Israel, and is surrounded by thick forest. From the crumbling towers and walls, there are impressive views of the flat Hula Valley to the south and the mountain pass between Hermon and Syria. Not surprisingly, the fortress once served as a highway stronghold along the road to Damascus but was abandoned after the fall of the Second Crusader Kingdom in 1291.

INTRODUCING ISRAEL

▲ *Above: The imposing Knesset in Jerusalem is Israel's parliament.*

Uncertain Times

Matters came to a head again in 1967, with a massive build-up of hostile troops along Israel's borders. After six days of fighting, previous ceasefire lines were replaced by new ones, with Judea, Samaria, Gaza, the Sinai Peninsula, and the Golan Heights under Israel's control. Jerusalem, which since 1949 had been divided under Israeli and Jordanian rule, was reunified under Israel's authority.

In 1973, several years of relative calm came to an end on Yom Kippur (the Day of Atonement), the holiest day of the Jewish year, when Egypt and Syria invaded Israel via the Suez Canal and the Golan Heights.

During the next three weeks, the **Israel Defense Forces (IDF)** turned the tide of battle and repulsed the attackers, crossing the Suez Canal into Egypt and advancing to within 32km (20 miles) of the Syrian capital, Damascus. It took two years of further negotiation before Israel withdrew.

In 1977, Egypt's President Sadat announced a desire for peace, and soon Begin extended the first olive branch to Sadat. In 1979 the **Camp David Accords** were signed, drawing up a framework for peace and self-government by the Palestinians. Israel withdrew from the Sinai.

However, ongoing fighting with **Lebanon** and sporadic episodes between Israel and the **Palestine Liberation Organization** (PLO) continued until 1985, when the last Israeli Defence Forces withdrew from Lebanon. A tentative peace settled for two years until the **Intifada**, a Palestinian uprising in Gaza and the West Bank, occurred. During the **Gulf War** (1990–91), the PLO sided with Iraq, and Israel feared attack by chemical weapons. Conventional missiles did hit Tel Aviv but Israel's lack of retaliation led to the establishment of diplomatic relations with a number of countries.

In September 1993 a new peace agreement was signed between **Yitzhak Rabin** and **Yasser Arafat** of the PLO. Under these **Oslo Accords**, Jericho and the Gaza Strip were granted a degree of Palestinian autonomy. Further cities were handed back to the Palestinians in 1994. In the same year, land borders opened between Jordan and the Israeli resort of Eilat in the south. However, Israeli prime minister Yitzhak Rabin was assassinated in November 1995 by a Jewish extremist and September 1996 saw further uprisings in Hebron and the Gaza Strip.

In 2000, there was a **second Intifada** with Palestinian attacks on Israeli civilians, further hampering the peace process. US president George W Bush was instrumental in the creation of a **Roadmap for Peace** in 2003, along with the UN, the EU and Russia, although it took until 2005 for this to have an impact. Meanwhile, in 2002, Israel began the construction of a massive security fence along areas bordering Palestinian territory, as protection of its citizens against terrorism, but alienated many Palestinians from the peace process. Israel disengaged from the Gaza Strip in 2005, evacuating its settlers and the IDF, though it maintained (and still does) control over the entry points. In 2006, the Palestinians elected **Hamas**, a Muslim extremist group, to head the Palestinian Legislative Council, once again freezing relations with Israel.

Ehud Olmert became Israel's prime minister in March 2006 and shelved plans to evacuate Israel's presence in most of the West Bank following an Israeli military operation in Gaza in June–July 2006 and a 34-day conflict with Hezbollah in Lebanon in June–August 2006.

Talks resumed with the Palestinian National Authority (PNA) after Hamas seized control of the Gaza Strip and PNA President **Mahmoud Abbas** formed a new government to oversee the West Bank without the Hamas militia. Ehud Olmert resigned in September 2008 and elections were held in 2009, resulting in a coalition between the Kadima and Likud parties. **Binyamin Netanyahu**, leader of the right-wing Likud Party, is currently Prime Minister.

As of early 2014, Israel remains in a state of tentative peace although periodic rocket-firing by the Palestinians and continuing construction on the West Bank leads to intermittent unrest. Meanwhile, US President Barack Obama continues to apply pressure on Binyamin Netanyahu to enter into peace negotiations with the Palestinians.

▲ *Above: Unexploded mines still lie in the Golan Heights.*

SERVING THEIR COUNTRY

The Israeli Defense Forces (IDF) is a source of national pride. All men and women are required at the age of 18 to do National Service. For men, this service lasts for three years but women are only required to do two years. From an even earlier age young people are assessed according to their suitability for divisions such as the paratroops, the Air Force or the infantry and tank corps. A career in the army is considered highly prestigious and it's a matter of considerable pride among many senior civilians that they once held posts as officers.

INTRODUCING ISRAEL

GOVERNMENT AND ECONOMY

Israel is a multiparty parliamentary democracy. The **Knesset**
(parliament) of 120 members is elected by proportional
representation from party lists, rather than individual can-
didates. The new leader of the party or coalition that has the
greatest chance of forming a government, usually with an
absolute majority, is invited by the existing president to do
so. The prime minister's election is slightly different, decided
by separate universal vote. The president, meanwhile, is
elected by the Knesset every five years by secret ballot. The
presidency is the highest office in Israel and the president
is considered to be above day-to-day politics but he does
appoint judges to the **Supreme Court**, which is the safeguard
of the country's democracy. The Supreme Court has the authority to intervene at all levels of life in Israel, from politics
to economic matters, and is held in enormous respect by the
people. Israelis are obsessed with politics and lively political
debate is part of everyday life, so be prepared to join in.

Israel has suffered from high **inflation** in the past, partly
due to the cost of maintaining its defence force; the country has one of the proportionally highest defence budgets
in the world. The economy, which has moved from agricultural to post-industrial, is relatively stable now with steady
growth, but life for the visitor is not cheap. Israel's main
exports include computer software, military equipment, cut
diamonds, chemicals and agricultural products. Roughly
half of the government's external debt is owed to the USA,
its major source of economic and military aid. The country's
income includes US$4.6 billion from tourism generated by
3 million visitors.

THE PEOPLE

If there was ever a cultural melting pot, Israel is it. Under
the **Law of Return**, any Jew, anywhere in the world, has
the right to live in Israel and take Israeli citizenship. This
is what has brought wave after wave of immigrants, from
the first Russians who arrived in 1882 to Germans, North
Africans and now, an estimated one million Soviet Jews,

looking for a new life of freedom after many years under Communism.

Israel's population is around 8.15 million. **Tel Aviv** has a population of 415,000, the total of its metropolitan area extending to 2.4 million. **Jerusalem**, meanwhile, has 815,000 residents. Israel's third city is **Haifa**, on the coast, with a more mixed Arab and Jewish population, and world centre of the Baha'i religion.

▲ *Above: Israel's flag bears the Star of David.*

Seventy-five per cent of the Israeli population is Jews, with 1.7 million Muslims and the rest Christians, Druze and others. While all these communities live and worship alongside one another, cultural boundaries remain clear and visitors will encounter second generation Armenians and Ethiopians who still speak as though they've just arrived in the country.

Native-born Israelis are nicknamed **sabras** – a cactus fruit which is tough and thorny on the outside and sweet on the inside – but in reality, Israelis are incredibly hospitable and naturally curious about visitors. Family ties are strong in Israel, and in Jewish families Friday nights are spent at home. Children are welcomed everywhere and usually stay up quite late.

Israelis are not big drinkers. A more typical night out consists of drinking coffee and talking. Young people are surprisingly mature, thanks to their three years' compulsory national service (two for girls), and tend to be great travellers and lovers of the outdoors.

Israeli people in general are hard-working, aggressive in business and highly demonstrative: shouting and gesticulating doesn't necessarily mean anger but rather discussion. Israelis are also immersed in politics, which is discussed endlessly on the radio, TV and in the many daily newspapers. By all means enter into a political discussion, but remember to have your argument well prepared.

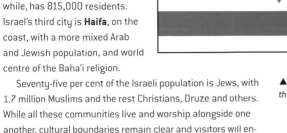

LANGUAGE OF THE EUROPEANS

Yiddish is a Germanic language written in Hebrew characters and spoken in Israel by mostly the older generation, particularly those with European roots. The language developed in southwestern Germany between the 9th and 12th centuries, as Hebrew words that pertained to Jewish religious life were added to German. Later, as Jews moved eastward into Slavic-speaking areas, some Slavic influences were added, in addition to Romanian, French and several English words. In the early years of the 20th century Yiddish was spoken by an estimated 11 million people in Eastern Europe and the USA, although the extermination of so many Jews in the Holocaust led to its decline.

INTRODUCING ISRAEL

▲ *Above: Muslims turn towards Mecca for the call to prayer.*

Language

The diversity of Israel's population is reflected in the number of languages you'll hear on the streets: **Hebrew**, **Yiddish**, **English**, **German**, **Arabic**, **French**, **Spanish**, **Amharic** (spoken by Ethiopian Jews) and a lot of **Russian**, spoken by recently arrived immigrants who now account for one-fifth of the population. Israel Radio broadcasts in no fewer than 12 different languages. Hebrew and Arabic, however, are the official languages, with English widely understood. Hebrew today is actually similar to biblical Hebrew, with an expanded vocabulary and a few English words thrown in. While the visitor can get by in virtually any language, it is only polite – and much appreciated by the locals – to learn a few words of Hebrew.

Few foreign-language television programmes are dubbed, so if you're learning Hebrew, watching TV is a perfect way to practise reading. Alternatively, there is plenty of choice in reading matter. Israel has around 20 daily newspapers, more than any other country in the world, published in Hebrew, Arabic, Russian and English. For English-speaking visitors, *The Jerusalem Post* is a good, if rather right-wing, read.

Religion

As well as forming the spiritual home of Judaism, Israel is the world's most important Christian site and is of great significance to Muslims. Israel is also home to Samaritans, Armenians, Eastern Orthodox adherents, and Druze; it forms the world headquarters of the Baha'i. Freedom of worship is guaranteed and, whatever your faith, you will be welcome. Of Israel's eight million-plus inhabitants, some 5.6 million are Jewish but only 20% of these claim to be 'practising'

SAMARITANS

The handful of Samaritans left in Israel today are descended from those mentioned in the Bible. By the time the Jews returned from Babylon, the Samaritans, who had stayed, had intermarried with the invaders and, while they adhered to the Jewish faith, were looked down on for not being pure. Strong antipathy arose between the two groups. The holiest site for Samaritans today is Mount Gerizim, where they once had a temple, later destroyed by the Hasmoneans. During Samaritan Passover, lambs are sacrificed here, although non-Samaritan spectators are asked to leave for the ritual.

Jews, which means daily prayer, religious observance of the Sabbath and keeping a kosher household.

Shabbat (the Sabbath) — sundown on Friday to sundown on Saturday — is a time of rest, contemplation and prayer and is strictly observed: exact times of sunset are published in the newspapers. Shops and restaurants close, offices are deserted, and public transport stops except in Tel Aviv and, to an extent, Haifa. In religious households, people don't cook or switch on any appliance, although nowadays electric timers are used to operate lights and food is prepared the day before and kept warm.

On Friday nights, traditional Shabbat supper is served. At sunset on Saturday, a *Havdalah* candle is lit to mark the passing of the holy day and a blessing is read. The family drinks a glass of kosher wine and passes round a pot of sweet-smelling spices or fresh herbs for everybody to inhale.

Shabbat need not affect the visitor. Chinese and Arab restaurants stay open and there is plenty of activity in the big hotels. In Tel Aviv, after supper, huge crowds turn out to stroll along the promenade in the warm night air.

Men in long black coats and black hats, with distinctive locks of hair around their faces, belong to the ultra-Orthodox sect, the devout **Hassidic Jews** who still dress as their original Eastern European predecessors did 200 years ago. They live in communities resembling the ghettos of the 1930s, the largest of which is Me'a She'arim in Jerusalem, almost recreating the conditions of the Eastern Europe they left behind, with narrow alleys and high, forbidding walls. Many of them do not serve in the army —although this may be enforced in the future — and furthermore, do not work, preferring to study the Scriptures instead.

Strangely, a number of Hassidic Jews do not even believe in the State of Israel. Their doctrine insists that the State of Israel will only exist after the coming of the Messiah, which they believe has not yet happened. Visitors to Me'a She'arim are politely warned at the entrance to dress with extreme modesty and not to disturb the residents.

THE SECT OF MYSTERY

The Druze are a mysterious sect of around 60,000 people, living in the mountains around Carmel, and are descended from an Egyptian religious movement of some 900 years ago. The men dress distinctively in a white headdress, black bloomers and cummerbund and they sport bushy moustaches. No-one knows exactly what Druze beliefs entail as they have been kept a secret through the generations, although reincarnation does play a part. Despite their enigmatic air, Druze are successfully integrated into Israeli society and unlike some sects — the Hassidim, for example — serve their time in the Israeli Defense Force.

INTRODUCING ISRAEL

▶ *Right: Worshippers celebrating Hanukkah.*

RELIGIOUS HOLIDAYS

January/February Tu B'Shevat: New Year for trees, with planting ceremonies.
March Purim: The Feast of Esther, with costume parades.
April Pesach or Passover: family celebration of the exodus from Egypt.
April/May Memorial Day: In memory of the Holocaust.
April/May Independence Day: Singing, dancing, picnics, carnivals and bonfires.
May Lag B'Omer: Pilgrimages and bonfires.
May/June Shavuot: Harvest festival of Pentecost.
July/August Tisha B'Av: Marks the destruction of the First and Second Temples.
Sept/Oct Rosh Hashanah: Jewish New Year, followed by Yom Kippur (Day of Atonement).
Sept/Oct Sukkot: The Feast of Tabernacles.
October Simchat Torah: Rejoicing of the Torah.
December Hanukkah: The Feast of Lights.

Festivals and Holidays

With so many different religions practised, life in Israel seems like one long holiday. The Christians observe Christmas and Easter, Muslims Ramadan and Jews the 13 holidays on the Jewish Calendar, which are 'official' as far as shops and businesses are concerned.

But Israelis will also celebrate New Year's Eve. The **Hebrew calendar** is based on the lunar year, so holiday dates do not follow the Gregorian calendar. God is said to have created the Earth in 3760BC, which corresponds to the Gregorian year 0. Thus 2009 is the year 5769, and so on.

Rosh Hashanah and Yom Kippur

Jewish New Year – Rosh Hashanah – falls in September or October. As the only two-day public holiday, this is the time when Israelis head for the beach, the Sea of Galilee or the mountains. For the religious, this is a time of self-examination. Ten days later is the **Day of Atonement**, or Yom Kippur, which is the holiest day of the year. Everything stops while the religious fast from sunset to sunset, and spend the day in the synagogue.

Sukkot and Simchat Torah

Sukkot, the **Harvest Festival,** is only a week or so after Yom Kippur. Every family builds a *succah*, a temporary shelter made of palm branches and leaves. Under its roof the family eats for seven days, commemorating the structures under which the Israelites lived during the exodus from Egypt. On the fifth day, there are parades and walks around Jerusalem. The last of the autumn vacations, the **Rejoicing of the Torah** (the first five books of the Bible), means singing and dancing in the streets with the **Torah Scroll**.

Hanukkah

The Feast of Lights in December celebrates the Jews recapturing their Holy Temple from the Greeks, who tried to suppress the Jewish faith. Hanukkah candles are lit on a menorah, the seven- or eight-branched candelabra owned by every household. Small jam-filled doughnuts are eaten everywhere, and children enjoy parties and games.

Passover

Passover, or Pesach, in March or April, celebrates the liberation of the ancient Israelites from Egypt. No bread or yeast is eaten for a week — just unleavened *matzot* — and people rid their houses of anything containing yeast, an excuse for a good spring clean. The Passover dinner, or *seder*, is a feast symbolizing the experiences of the Israelites as they fled from Egypt, including bitter herbs representing the bitterness of slavery.

Traditional Cultures

Dance, art and theatre are prolific in Israel and there are cultural performances everywhere, from the smallest kibbutz to the theatre stages of Jerusalem and Tel Aviv. As well as classical ballet, dance incorporates several ethnic styles, such as Hassidic, Arabic and Yemenite folk dancing. **BatSheva** and the **Kibbutz Contemporary Dance Co.** are modern dance companies that perform regularly nationally and internationally.

The Arts

Israel's magnificent landscapes have inspired countless painters and there are large artistic communities in **Jaffa**, the village of **Ein Hod** near Haifa and **Safed** in the Galilee

INTRODUCING ISRAEL

▲ *Above: Relaxing at the sunny resort of Eilat by the Red Sea.*
▶ *Opposite: In Tel Aviv you can windsurf off the white-sand beaches.*

region. Important galleries include the **Israel Museum** in Jerusalem, which houses works of contemporary Israeli art, Jewish European art and sculpture, a vast number of European works and also a modern section. In Tel Aviv, don't miss the city's **Museum of Art**, with its outstanding contemporary collection. The wonderful **Helena Rubenstein Pavilion** also includes European and American art from the 17th to the 20th centuries.

The **Israel Philharmonic Orchestra** is world famous and often features well-known guest performers. The orchestra's home is the **Mann Auditorium** in Tel Aviv and tickets are usually hard to come by. In Jerusalem, try to see the **Jerusalem Symphony Orchestra**, which performs weekly throughout the winter. Its home is the Henry Crown Hall at the beautiful **Jerusalem Centre for the Performing Arts**.

There are numerous theatre groups in Tel Aviv and Jerusalem, although if you're travelling around, nothing quite beats the romance of theatre at dusk in the beautiful Roman amphitheatre at Caesarea, 50km (30 miles) from Tel Aviv, as the sun sets across the waves. There are theatre performances here as well as an annual jazz festival. In Tel Aviv, the **Habima Theatre** is the home of the National Theatre of Israel, while performances are also staged at the **Suzanne Dellal Centre** for Dance and Theatre at Neve Tzedek. The city's flagship venue, though, is the **Tel Aviv Performing Arts Centre**, home to the famous Israeli Opera. Jerusalem has several theatres, the main one being the Jerusalem Centre for the Performing Arts.

Also worth a visit is the **Red Sea Jazz Festival** (Eilat) in both February and August and the **Akko Fringe Theatre Festival** in September/October. In spring, the **Rubenstein International Piano Master Competition** attracts talent from all over the world.

FABULOUS FESTIVALS

Not to be confused with religious holidays, there are numerous colourful cultural festivals in the Israeli calendar.
February/August: Jazz Festival.
March: Ein Gev Music Festival; classical and folk music is played at the Kibbutz Ein Gev on the Sea of Galilee.
June: Israel Festival – (international festival of music and dance).
August: Klezmer Festival, Safed (instrumental music).
September: International Classical Guitar Festival, Netanya.
October: Haifa International Film Festival.

Nightlife

Tel Aviv has the liveliest nightlife, with a cutting-edge lounge bar and club scene to rival Ibiza or Ayia Napa, only cooler. The new **Tel Aviv Port** and **Lilienblum Street** are the hottest spots for nightlife. Pop concerts are held in Tel Aviv's Ha-Yarkon Park, under the stars. Jerusalem has a lively café society and a growing bar and club scene in the side streets off the **Jaffa Road**, **the Russian Compound** and **Talpiot Industrial Zone**. **Eilat** is a more typical holiday resort with a mixture of clubs and pubs focusing on the big hotels on North Beach.

Sport in Israel

Israelis are generally active, outdoor types and there are countless opportunities to indulge in sports from the everyday to the extreme.

Hiking is very popular, some of the best areas being the Negev Desert and the Galilee region. In the Negev, there are marked trails in the national parks like Ein Gedi, overlooking the Dead Sea, although many locals prefer to hike away from the tourist areas, camping out overnight. **Mountain biking**, rappelling (abseiling) and off-road driving are all popular in this area, too.

Around the Sea of Galilee, there are gentle walking trails taking in the religious sites and others covering more remote areas, including the spectacular Golan Heights. A guide is essential outside the designated park areas on the Golan Heights as danger still exists from unexploded landmines.

Water sports abound around the lake, from water skiing to canoeing. **White-water rafting** is popular on the River Jordan, which is rated as one of the most exciting in the world.

For a gentler experience, try **inner tubing**; in other words, drifting down a quiet

INTRODUCING ISRAEL

▲ *Above: One of east Jerusalem's many popular bakeries.*
▶ *Opposite: For excellent dishes in a splendid setting, Jaffa's restaurants are hard to beat.*

KEEPING KOSHER

'Kosher' comes from the Hebrew *kasher*, meaning 'fit' or 'proper'. It is applied especially to the food that Jews are permitted to eat. According to the Bible only animals that have cloven hooves and are ruminant (that is, chew the cud) are considered kosher. These animals must be killed according to the traditional rabbinical ritual and soaked, salted, and washed to remove any traces of blood. Milk or milk products must not be eaten with meat, and shellfish is to be avoided. During the Passover Festival, only unleavened bread is to be eaten.

stretch of the river sitting in a rubber tube, soaking up the peace and quiet.

Horse riding is also very popular and some of the best rides are from ranches located around the lake. Horses tend to be trained Western-style and many have thoroughbred blood.

A visit to Eilat is an ideal opportunity to try **scuba diving** in the Red Sea's warm, clear waters with their spectacular coral reefs. A starter course takes just one day. For those who prefer not to dive, the snorkelling is almost as good. On the Mediterranean coast, meanwhile, sea kayaking and sailing are popular sports.

Food and Drink

A biblical law that 'a kid shall not seethe in its mother's milk' led to the rule that meat and milk should not be mixed. A kosher restaurant or home will keep two sets of crockery and utensils, one for milk and one for meat. Scavenging creatures like pigs and shellfish are considered unclean and are not eaten, although all sorts of crafty imitations do appear, like 'prawns' and crabsticks made of fish. Many Jews (Orthodox) will eat vegetarian food in a restaurant where the kosher observance is uncertain. Coming to terms with all the complexities of kosher and non-kosher takes a while but most visitors are amazed at the variety they find in Israeli cuisine: a breakfast buffet groaning under cheese platters and mounds of fruit or a candlelit feast of *chateaubriand* washed down with a very palatable red wine.

Many restaurants and most hotels observe Jewish law, selling either meat or dairy products, but never both. A meat restaurant will serve margarine – not butter – non-dairy cream and no cheese sauces. Vegetarians will love the dairy restaurants, which are great for pasta, delicious cheeses, salad bars and creamy desserts. Most hotels have one outlet of each type.

'Typical' Israeli cuisine does not really exist. Like the people, Israeli food is a collection of cultures. If anything does typify eating in Israel, however, it's dishes from the Middle East region, which include falafel – tiny balls of chickpea, deep fried and stuffed into pitta bread — with salad; hummus, a garlicky chickpea dip; and smooth *tahini*, a paste made of sesame seeds. Kebabs of veal, chicken, lamb or beef are sold everywhere, usually with a vast salad. Try the *harif*, a spicy condiment that peps up the blandest falafel Eastern European cooking, often regarded (wrongly) as 'typical' Jewish food,

features in some Israeli homes: *gefilte* fish, chopped liver, borscht and Hungarian goulash.

Fish is sold everywhere. Grilled sardines are served on the beaches, and fishermen in Galilee still bring in plump, freshwater trout and the tasty St Peter fish, as they did in biblical times.

Of course, not all restaurants are kosher. An influx of Chinese, Vietnamese and Filipinos has led to the establishment of many Asian restaurants, with pork and prawns in abundance. Israel has its fair share of fast-food outlets, too, particularly in the big cities.

Fruit in Israel is magnificent and the markets have spectacular fruit displays. Kiwi, mango, pomegranate, passion fruit, custard apple and papaya are grown here, as are the world's largest strawberries and endless varieties of citrus.

Fruit juices from street vendors are wonderfully refreshing. Coffee is served black, strong and sweet (Turkish) or creamy and frothy (Viennese). *Botz* is the strong Israeli version of Turkish coffee.

Israelis are not big drinkers but the country produces some good wines (red and white) from the Carmel region, the Galilee and Rishon leZion, southeast of Tel Aviv. Local beers, bottled and draft, are available, and the local aniseed-flavoured firewater is called *arak*.

FESTIVAL NOSH

On Hannukah, small jam doughnuts, or *sufganiot*, are eaten throughout Israel, as well as *latkes*, or potato pancakes. In January or February on Arbour Day, families eat fruit from biblical times such as olives, dates, pomegranates and figs. During Passover, everybody eats unleavened bread, in the form of wafers which are baked for a short time only. The tradition stems from when Moses and the Israelites fled from Egypt — there was no time to leave the bread to rise, so they ate flat loaves. Tastier Passover fare includes coconut macaroons. If you dine with a Jewish family on Shabbat, expect *cholent*, a bean and meat stew that is baked on Friday.

2
Jerusalem

Exploring the walled **Old City** of Jerusalem is like peeling back layers of an onion; history unfolds as you descend from the bustling modern streets through time to the pillars and columns of the Roman era, 2000 years old, yet still standing under the buildings today.

Christians, Jews and Muslims have made Jerusalem their spiritual home and church bells ring as the haunting call to prayer echoes across rooftops from minarets. Visit the gold-domed mosque, the **Dome of the Rock**, or follow in what Christians believe to be Jesus' footsteps along the **Via Dolorosa** to the **Church of the Holy Sepulchre**, marking the spot of the crucifixion, burial and resurrection. Watch the devout praying at the **Western Wall**, the most sacred location for the Jewish faith.

Many faiths live in peace in war-ravaged Jerusalem, even sharing the same church in some cases. People are endlessly colourful, with sombre **Hassidic Jews**, chattering **Muslim Quarter** market stallholders, and awe-struck pilgrims soaking up the city's incredible atmosphere.

Jerusalem falls into three areas. The **Jewish West**, regarded by Israelis as their country's capital, is a busy, modern city and the seat of government (the Knesset). **Occupied East Jerusalem**, largely Arab, contains mosques, low-rise sandstone houses and fascinating biblical sites like the **Mount of Olives** and the **Garden of Gethsemane**. At the heart of Jerusalem is the walled **Old City** (parts of it are 3000 years old) which is a magnet to visitors from all over the world.

TOP ATTRACTIONS

★★★ **Via Dolorosa:** walk in the last footsteps of Jesus.
★★★ **Yad Vashem:** a moving Holocaust memorial.
★★★ **The Western Wall:** the holiest site in the world for Jews.
★★ **The Shrine of the Book:** houses the Dead Sea Scrolls which are the oldest documents known to man.
★★ **Arab Quarter:** shopping heaven.
★★ **The Church of the Holy Sepulchre:** visit the heart of the Christian religion.

◄ *Opposite: The magnificently tiled Dome of the Rock.*

JERUSALEM

▶ *Opposite top: Jerusalem's fortified walls, studded with gates, encircle the city for over two miles.*

THE OLD CITY

Jerusalem's walled Old City is probably the most important site in Israel. The honey-coloured walls, which snake around the cluster of narrow streets and magnificent churches and temples for over two miles, are remarkably intact considering that they are over 400 years old. The Turkish ruler **Suleiman the Magnificent** was responsible for most of what remains

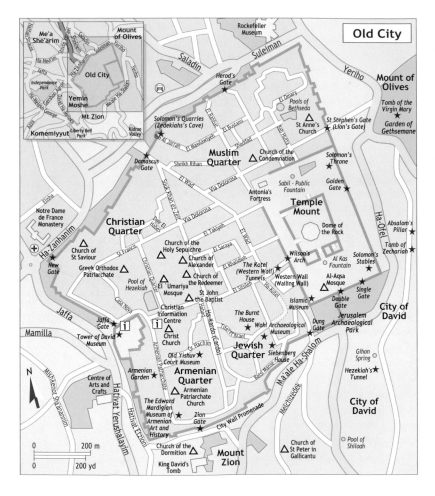

today of the walls, constructed during 1538–41. Other parts date back to the **Crusaders**, and others even further back to **King Herod**. The walls, represent, literally, layer upon layer of history.

There are eight gates to the Old City, seven of which are open to people and cars. Belief has it that the eighth, the **Golden Gate** (sealed by the Muslims in the 7th century), will only open on Judgement Day. The gates are all known by their Arab, Jewish and English names. Moving clockwise along the northern wall, the first gate is the **Damascus Gate**, one of the most impressive Islamic buildings around. It is open from 09:00–16:00 Monday–Thursday, Saturday and Sunday; 09:00–14:00 Friday. About 100m (328ft) east is **Herod's Gate**, restored in mid-2010, where the Crusaders broke through the city walls in July 1099. It was mistakenly believed that Herod Antipas's palace was nearby, hence the gate's name.

St Stephen's Gate, named after the first Christian martyr who was stoned to death here, leads to the Mount of Olives and Gethsemane. The **Golden Gate** (the sealed entrance leading to the Temple Mount) is where, according to Christians, the Messiah will enter the city. The **Dung Gate**, the smallest of the gates, was so named because the area around this gate was once a rubbish dump! Parts of the **Zion Gate** had to be pulled down to give access to a Franciscan monastery that hadn't been incorporated within the city's walls.

The **Jaffa Gate** is important as it marked the point of arrival for people travelling from the ancient port of Jaffa. Lastly, the **New Gate** (opened in 1887) was built mainly to give access from the pilgrim hospices to the Christian holy sites of the Old City.

▼ *Below: Jaffa Gate is a prominent entrance to the Old City.*

JERUSALEM

THE OLD CITY IN A DAY

With a car, it's possible to do a whistle-stop tour of the Old City and its surrounds. First, go through the Jaffa Gate to the Armenian Quarter, then use the Zion Gate which leads to the Jewish Quarter. Walk the Cardo, visit the Western Wall and the Temple Mount. Then walk the Via Dolorosa to the Holy Sepulchre. By car, visit the Garden Tomb, drive round the walls to the Garden of Gethsemane and up to the Mount of Olives to admire the view. Finish the tour at Absalom's Tomb at the top of the Kidron Valley.

▶ *Opposite: The Cardo was once the city's principal thoroughfare.*
▼ *Below: The Tower of David Museum highlights Jerusalem's history.*

The Tower of David Museum ★★★

Just inside **Jaffa Gate**, opposite the tourist information office, is one of the city's most important museums, the **Tower of David**. It's almost essential to start here if you have not been to Israel or Jerusalem before; the carefully planned multimedia exhibit tells the story of Jerusalem from its very origins, with bas relief models, archaeological exhibits and thoughtfully arranged panels for a quick visit, or audiovisual for a longer, more detailed tour. The museum itself is housed in a series of guard rooms of the old citadel. The views over the Old City from the top of the ramparts are breathtaking. Open Sun–Thu 09:00–16:00, Fri–Sat 09:00–14:00 (Jul–Aug Sat–Thu 09:00–17:00). Guided tours in English Sun–Thu at 11:00. Sound and Light show Mon, Wed and Thu 19:30 and 20:30, Sat 20:00 and 21:00. Times subject to change.

Ramparts Walk ★★★

Walking part of the ramparts surrounding the Old City is a delightful way of looking down on life on either side of the walls. You can start either at the Tower of David or from the **Damascus Gate** and wind your way around the massive fortifications, walking along the top. There are amazing views of **Yemin Moshe** suburb and West Jerusalem, several major Old City Christian churches including the **Church of the Dormition**, a rare glimpse inside the cloistered **Armenian Quarter**, the Valley of Hinnom and, on a clear day, vistas as far afield as the **Judean Desert**.

The Damascus Gate section allows walkers to observe the bustle of the **Arab market** below, the green oasis of the **Garden of Gethsemane** and its beautiful churches, the ancient cemetery on the **Mount of Olives** and the rooftops of the **Muslim Quarter**. The Jaffa Gate path ends near the Dung Gate, and the Damascus Gate path ends at St Stephen's Gate. Nobody is allowed to walk on the wall near the Western Wall. Open 09:00–16:00 Sun–Thu and Sat; 09:00–14.00 Fri.

The Armenian Quarter ★★

A quiet quarter of the Old City, the Armenian sector has a hushed atmosphere, with priests in flowing black robes and grey beards moving noiselessly along the dark, narrow and ancient streets. Nestled under the wall to the right of the Tower of David, this area is nonetheless worth exploring for its tiny churches, ancient buildings and green, hidden courtyards.

The Jewish Quarter ★★★

In the southeast corner of the city, bordered by the Armenian Quarter, the Western Wall and Hashalshelet Street, the Jewish Quarter's well-laid-out streets have been inhabited since the 8th century BC – but sadly destroyed many times. Today, the area is a peaceful oasis of smart shops, synagogues, street cafés and apartments, an ideal rest stop before plunging into the chaos of the Arab Quarter (see page 39).

The Cardo ★★

Walk along the Cardo, a fascinating Roman street, laid down in the 6th century as the city's main thoroughfare. At various points, you can look down through glass sections at the ancient cobbled road and the remnants of arches and buildings from over 1400 years ago. There are elements of Ottoman, Crusader and Byzantine architecture, the oldest sections of the excavations below the street dating back to the 8th century BC. Lines of bricks laid into the stone underfoot indicate the outline of former streets – orange bricks depict

JEWISH ETIQUETTE

- Men and boys should wear a *kippa*, or skullcap, in a synagogue, at the Western Wall, at the Yad Vashem Holocaust Memorial, and at funerals. Normally, a *kippa* can be borrowed from the synagogue or site.
- Do not take photographs of the Western Wall on *Shabbat*; it is considered to be offensive.
- Modest dress is appropriate in religious places, particularly Me'a She'arim, where arms, legs and heads should not be exposed.
- In Tel Aviv's Orthodox suburb of Bnei Brak and certain areas of Jerusalem, no traffic is allowed on *Shabbat* and cars may be stoned.
- You can spend a Friday evening with an ultra-Orthodox family. Ask at tourist offices or at the Western Wall for information.

JERUSALEM

▲ *Above: Men and women pray separately at the Western Wall.*

a street from the 8th century BC and black bricks the 1st century BC.

Alone on the Walls Museum ★

This tiny photographic exhibit tells the story of the fall of the Jewish Quarter in 1948, as recorded by the American **John Philips**, a photojournalist who was in Jerusalem as a correspondent for *Life* magazine for the whole battle. Beautifully shot, the images are both graphic and moving. The museum was opened on the 40th anniversary of the liberation of Jerusalem, in 2007. Open 09:00–17:00 Sun–Thu, 09:00–13:00 Fri.

Wohl Archaeological Museum ★

This is a fascinating archaeological site in Hakara'im Street, giving a clear insight into the lives of Jerusalem's nobility during the **Second Temple Period**. The site comprises six houses, discovered when the Jewish Quarter was being renovated in 1967, with three of them on display. Beautiful mosaics and frescoes were found and you'll see all sorts of other signs of great wealth: storage rooms, reservoirs for water, ritual baths, stoneware for serving food, terracotta tableware, amphorae that would have contained wine, and delicate flasks. The rooms were spacious, some with balconies, and archaeologists have confirmed that the buildings would have been two storeys high. Open 09:00–17:00 Sun–Thu, 09:00–13:00 Fri.

The Burnt House ★★

Would-be archaeologists should call in at the Burnt House on Tiferet Israel Street, where there's a fascinating audiovisual show of the excavations of the Jewish Quarter. This luxurious

CONQUESTS OF ALLENBY

War hero Viscount Allenby (1861–1936) was born in Felixstowe, England, and educated at the Royal Military Academy, Sandhurst. Allenby was assigned in 1917 as commander-in-chief of the Egyptian Expeditionary Force. He led an offensive against the Turkish armies in the Middle East, capturing Jerusalem on 9 December 1917, winning decisively at Megiddo in September 1918, and taking Damascus on 1 October 1918. The campaign forced the Turks to retreat and Allenby was promoted to the rank of field marshal. From 1919–25 he was British high commissioner in Egypt. The main Israel/Jordan border crossing, the Allenby Bridge, is named after him.

house belonged to a religious family in the **Second Temple Period** 538BC–AD70 (when the Jewish exiles returned from Babylon and rebuilt the Temple) but was burnt in AD70 along with the rest of Jerusalem. Its sooty remains are better preserved than many of the other buildings and it has been converted into a museum. It is open 09:00–17:00 Sun–Thu and 09:00–13:00 Fri.

The Western Wall ★★★

The Western Wall, or the **Kotel**, is the holiest site in the whole of Jerusalem to Jews, who believe it to be the last remnant of the Temple that housed the **Ark of the Covenant**. The plaza in front of the remaining exposed section of the Wall is one of the city's most famous sights, divided into a men's and a women's area, where Jews from all over the world come to pray.

Visitors can go up to the Wall, although you must be appropriately dressed. It is best to avoid Friday afternoons, when a lot of Orthodox Jews come to pray, many of whom do not appreciate the attention of tourists, and cameras should be used with great discretion. Monday is a good day to visit, when a lot of **Bar Mitzvahs** take place and you may see long processions, some with musical accompaniment, and large groups dressed in white to celebrate the occasion. It is customary to place your prayer to God on a piece of paper and slip it between the ancient stones. Open 24 hours a day.

Western Wall Tunnels ★★★

A relatively new attraction and a controversial one is the **Western Wall Tunnels**, an amazing piece of excavation that extends the entire 488 metres (534yd) of the Wall, underground, deep below the modern city, revealing stone-work from **Herod**'s time. You'll pass ancient **cisterns**, water courses and **quarries** and at one point, a tiny section of the Wall itself, usually occupied with four or five women praying (this section allows them to get closer to the holiest part of the Wall than the women's section of the exposed area in the Plaza). During the walk through the narrow tunnels, you can appreciate the enormous scale of the excavation, with

---

THE INN OF THE GOOD SAMARITAN

The Parable of the Good Samaritan in *Luke* tells of the wounded Jew who was ignored by other travellers, most of them Samaritans, once sworn enemies of the Jews. However, one Samaritan stopped to help the traveller and took him to an inn. Although the story is fiction, a sign marks the spot, some 10km (6 miles) from the Mount of Olives on the Jericho Road, where the inn was supposed to have been. As traveller's inns were commonplace in the first century, the likelihood of some kind of building having existed here is strong.

OPENING HOURS IN JERUSALEM

Note that although specific opening and closing times are given for the various religious sites, these are subject to change. They are dependent on political circum- stances, and also vary be- tween summer and winter due to longer or shorter days of sunlight.

sudden drop-offs down through even more layers of history or glances up through the stone ceiling to vast, hidden caverns. The tunnels start at the Western Wall Plaza and emerge on Lion's Gate Road by a Muslim school. Visits take place in groups (book well advance on tel: 972 2 627 1333, www.thekotel.org). Don't visit if you are claustrophobic or heavily overweight – the tunnels are extremely narrow and you may encounter groups coming the other way. It's hot, too. Open 07:00 until evening, depending on bookings, Sun–Thu; 07:00–12:00 Fri.

Temple Mount ★★★

The Temple Mount is sacred to Muslims as it is believed to be the site from which **Mohammed the Prophet** ascended to heaven. The **Dome of the Rock**, that magnificent gold dome that is so prominent on the Jerusalem skyline, is built over the spot where Abraham is believed to have prepared his son, Isaac, for sacrifice (Abraham is an important historical figure in Muslim belief too), which is also the site of the **First Temple**. Muslims pay homage to a small enclosure where there's a footprint of Mohammed, and some hairs from his beard. There is also a handprint, believed to be that of the **Archangel Gabriel**, who held down the rock as Mohammed ascended. The silver-coloured **Al-Aqsa Mosque**, built to commemorate the furthest point that Mohammed travelled from Mecca, is the third most holy site to Muslims after Mecca and Medina. Non-Muslims are not allowed in the mosque but are welcome on tours of the compound, which features many superb examples of Islamic art

▼ *Below: Muslims outside the Dome of the Rock on Temple Mount.*

◀ *Left: Although the details of the construction of Al-Aqsa Mosque are a matter of dispute, the mosque can accommodate up to 5000 worshippers for prayer.*
▼ *Below: View over the Arab Quarter of the Old City, with its fascinating market streets.*

and architecture, minarets, tiles and artwork. Open Sat–Thu 07:30–11:00 and 12:00–13:30, although times vary between summer and winter. The Temple Mount is closed on all Christian, Jewish or Muslim holidays and any other days considered 'sensitive' by the Muslim custodians of the site. Many Jews do not wish to come here for fear of treading on a sacred part of the Temple. You will need a passport as ID in order to visit.

The Arab Quarter ★★

After the open skies of the Temple Mount, take a deep breath and plunge into the chaotic sights, sounds and smells of the Arab Quarter. Two streets, **Souq Khan ez-Zeit** and **El Wad**, are traditional *souqs*, or markets, packed with trinkets, brass, Armenian tiles, Palestinian pottery, leather (often rather rancid and untreated), carvings and antiques. Some stalls sell huge piles of nuts; others are pungent with spices in brilliant reds and yellows. Sticky *baklava*, dripping with honey, and chunks of nougat are popular snacks. Carpets, clothing and gold-embroidered fabrics suspended over the narrow streets mean it's always dark in the *souq*; you'll be shouted at, pursued by enthusiastic stallholders and hassled from all

angles. If you seriously intend buying anything, haggling is essential.

The Christian Quarter ★★★

The Christian Quarter occupies the northwest corner of the walled city, its focal point the **Church of the Holy Sepulchre**. In the maze of narrow but clean and orderly streets, the best and most popular route to follow is the **Via Dolorosa**, or the Way of the Cross, the route believed by Christians to have been taken by Jesus from the **Praetorium** where he was condemned to death to **Calvary** where he was crucified. Groups of pilgrims move slowly along the narrow road, stopping to pray at each of the 14 stations (the stops Jesus made along the Via Dolorosa), many of them unable to believe that they are actually in Jerusalem, following Jesus' footsteps. Somewhat less spiritual is the rampant commercialism that pervades the area, with the endless tacky souvenir shops and boutiques lining the route.

Via Dolorosa ★★★

Because Jerusalem has so many layers, the Via Dolorosa is unlikely to be the precise path that Jesus walked. The original is probably hidden under 2000 years of subsequent building. However, when the route and surrounding buildings were given a facelift, large slabs of stone were revealed along the way, believed to date back to Roman times. The route begins in the Arab Quarter, just inside **St Stephen's Gate**, and

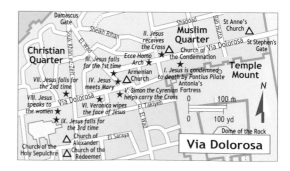

Via Dolorosa

the 'Stations of the Cross' are illuminated for night-time visitors. Guided tours operate daily from the Pilgrim's Reception Plaza opposite **St Anne's Church**, a Crusader church which marks Mary's birthplace, and the **Pools of Bethesda**, where Jesus healed the cripple.

The **First Station of the Cross**, where Pilate sentenced Jesus to death, is in the courtyard of the **Umariyah School**. The actual setting is believed to have been Herod's Antonia Fortress, the foundations now covered by the churches lining the Via Dolorosa. The **Ecce Homo Arch** outside the Church of the Sisters of Zion takes its name from Pilate's sneer at Jesus, 'Behold the man'.

The **Second Station**, where Jesus received his cross and had a crown of thorns placed on his head, is opposite the Franciscan Church of the Condemnation. The **Third**, which marks his first fall, is at the point where Via Dolorosa crosses the street El Wad. The **Fourth Station**, where Jesus met his mother, Mary, is marked by an Armenian Church. At the **Fifth Station**, Simon the Cyrenian helped Jesus carry the cross. The House of St Veronica marks the **Sixth**, where Veronica wiped Jesus' face with her veil.

The Via Dolorosa then bisects the souq Kahn ez-Zeit, the location of the **Seventh Station**, where Jesus fell for the second time.

Two more stations lie outside the Church of the Holy Sepulchre. The **Eighth** is marked by a Greek Orthodox chapel, St Charalambous, built over the spot where Jesus spoke to the women of Jerusalem: 'Weep not for me, but for Jerusalem.' A pillar marks the point at which he fell a third time – the **Ninth Station**. The remaining five stations are contained within the Church of the Holy Sepulchre.

Church of the Holy Sepulchre ★★★

The squat Church of the Holy Sepulchre, the heart of the Christian Quarter, covers **Calvary** (**Golgotha** in Hebrew), the Place of the Skull. Much of the present structure dates from the 12th century, built by the Crusaders, although a place of worship has stood here since the 4th century.

HOLY TEACHINGS

The bibles of Judaism and Christianity are different. The Jewish Bible consists of the Old Testament, 39 books originally written in Hebrew, except for a few sections which are written in Aramaic (the ancient language of the Middle East). The Christian Bible is comprised of two parts: the Old Testament and the 27 Books of the New Testament (originally written in Greek). The Old Testament is structured in two slightly different forms by Catholics and Protestants. Roman Catholics use the Jewish Bible plus seven other books and additions; Protestants limit it to the 39 books of the Jewish Bible.

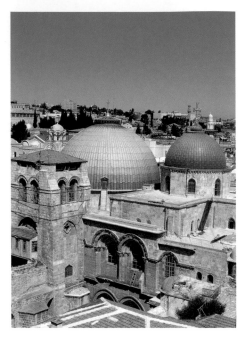

The Holy Sepulchre is actually a cluster of five churches, some with a bigger part of the communal space than others. For visitors, it's difficult to distinguish between Armenian and Greek Orthodox, Syrian Orthodox, Roman Catholic and Abyssinian Coptic, and there's always a service going on somewhere in the maze, chanting in different languages, the air heavy with incense and bearded priests scuttling backwards and forwards in the dim light.

Hapless tourists are bound to shuffle around the remaining five stations in slow-moving lines. To grasp the significance of each area, enlisting a professional guide is a good idea.

Inside the door, up a flight of steps, is Golgotha and the **10th Station**, where Jesus was stripped. A mosaic in the floor tells the story.

The next three stations, located close together and marked by altars, attract large crowds. Here Jesus was nailed to the Cross, the Cross was hoisted upright, and his body was later taken down.

The final, **14th Station** is the Holy Sepulchre itself. The marble tomb below contains the rock that guarded the entrance, the burial site, and the tomb of **Joseph of Arimathea**. Open Mon–Sat 08:30–17:30. Tours are available with advance notice.

EAST JERUSALEM
The Mount of Olives ★★★
The Mount of Olives, rising up behind the Old City in East Jerusalem, is the best place to go for spectacular views. Sunrise and sunset are the most beautiful times.

GLOSSARY

• *Aliyah*: a wave of immigrants. The first was 1882–1903. A new Aliyah began at the beginning of the 1990s, as Israel accommodated thousands of Russian Jews in search of a new life.
• *Diaspora*: the dispersal of Jews all over the world and their efforts to maintain their religion and culture while displaced.
• *Shabbat*: the Sabbath, from sunset on Friday to sunset on Saturday.
• *Kibbutz*: a collective farm or village with communal ownership, inhabited by kibbutzniks.
• *Souq*: an Arab-style market.
• *Wadi*: a seasonal river bed.

The olive-less hill is steeped in legend and belief. The **Jewish cemetery**, still in use, dates back to biblical times and is considered the most sacred in the world. Jesus is believed to have entered Jerusalem from the Mount of Olives, through the Golden Gate, now sealed until the arrival of the next Messiah. Jews and Christians believe that a second Messiah will resurrect the dead and lead them once again through the gate, so the Mount of Olives is in great demand as a burial site. Muslims also believe that the dead will rise here on the **Day of Judgement** and the section below the city walls is the Muslim cemetery.

▲ *Above: The cemetery on the Mount of Olives is much in demand.*
◄ *Opposite: The Holy Sepulchre is home to five religions in all.*

Dome of the Ascension ★

The rocky slopes of the Mount of Olives are dotted with churches, some spectacular, some modest. The small Dome of the Ascension marks the spot from which Jesus is believed to have ascended to heaven. There has been a church here since AD390, later a Crusader church and, from the 17th century, a mosque and minaret were added. The site is of significance because of the presence of a slab of rock believed to bear the footprint of Jesus (Jesus' ascension is recognized by Islam, although the event does not appear in the Qur'an). If the door is closed, you can ring the bell to gain access.

Church of Mary Magdalene ★★

One of the most beautiful churches, with its seven golden domes, this **Russian Orthodox** church was built in 1888 by Tsar Alexander III. Inside the church there are beautiful wall paintings and sumptuous icons in gold and jewel-like colours, typical of the Russian Orthodox style. Open Tue and Thu 10:00–12:00.

JERUSALEM

▶ *Right: The Church of All Nations is designed in the Byzantine style.*
▶▶ *Opposite: A number of Israel's gnarled olive trees, seen here in the Garden of Gethsemane, are believed to date back to the time of Jesus.*

Church of All Nations ★★

The contemporary **Church of All Nations** stands at the foot of the Mount of Olives, next to the peaceful **Garden of Gethsemane**. The church, also known as the **Basilica of the Agony**, was built between 1919 and 1924, funded by 12 countries, hence the reference to 'All Nations'. It was designed by Antonio Barluzzi in a Byzantine style, with sturdy pillars, a domed roof and floor mosaics, and it has a dazzling and powerful mosaic on the façade depicting Jesus as a link between man and God. Inside, the symbols of the countries that built the church are inlaid in the ceilings of the 12 gold cupolas.

The church is run by Franciscans (Catholic) but has an Anglican service in the garden on Maundy Thursday, the day before Good Friday. Open Mon–Sat, 08:00–12:00 and 14:00–17:30, but times change seasonally.

Garden of Gethsemane ★

Next to the Church of All Nations, at the foot of the hill, is the Garden of Gethsemane where Jesus was betrayed and arrested. The gnarled olive trees in the garden are believed to be up to 2000 years old, although they are unlikely to be from the exact time of Christ as the Romans are believed to

JESUS CHRIST SUPERSTAR

The name Jesus is derived from a Greek version of the Hebrew name Joshua (or Yehoshuah, meaning 'Jehovah is deliverance'). The title 'Christ' comes from the Greek word, Christos, a translation of the Hebrew, Mashiakh or Messiah. 'Christ' was used by Jesus' early followers, who regarded him as the promised deliverer of Israel and later it was included as part of Jesus' proper name by the church, which regards him as the redeemer of all humanity.

have destroyed all the olive trees around Jerusalem during the **siege of AD70**. Still, the trees are impressively ancient and the garden is a peaceful place for quiet contemplation. It is open 08:00–12:00 and 14:00–18:00 daily (summer).

Mary's Tomb ★

A path to the left of the garden leads underground to the candlelit tombs of the Virgin Mary's parents, **Anne** and **Joachim**. Some believe that the 5th-century chapel also contains the remains of Mary herself and her husband, Joseph, although the Bible provides no accurate account of the end of Mary's life or the place of her burial. Open 06:00–12:00 and 14:30–17:00 daily.

Church of Dominus Flevit ★

This is another modern church, shaped by architect **Antonio Barluzzi** as a tear drop, commemorating the spot where Jesus in the Bible approached Jerusalem and wept as he predicted that the city would be 'dashed to the ground' (which it was, in AD70). The church is built over earlier remains

Israel calls Jerusalem its capital but the **United Nations** does not recognize this, and most countries that have relations with Israel have an embassy in Tel Aviv and a consulate in Jerusalem. The 1949 Armistice Line, or Green Line, as it's sometimes called, goes straight through the city, skimming the western side of the Old City. East of the line is 'East Jerusalem', the predominantly Arab neighbourhood annexed by Jordan after the 1949 Armistice and held by them until their defeat in the 1967 Six Day War, when Israel reunited the city. Since 1980 Israel has greatly expanded the municipal boundaries of Jerusalem, taking in Arab villages, but also building new Jewish neighbourhoods. The population of the expanded Jerusalem east of the Green Line is now approximately 238,000 Arabs and 190,000 Jews. The United Nations and others regard East Jerusalem as 'occupied territory'. A key demand of the Palestinian Authority has been that East Jerusalem should be the capital of an independent Palestinian state – a position that to date has been unacceptable to Israel because East Jerusalem includes the Western Wall, Temple Mount and the Jewish Quarter of the Old City as well as the new Jewish districts.

JERUSALEM

PLACE NAMES

The variety of names for each place is hardly surprising, given the number of different factions that have settled in Israel over time.

• **Jerusalem** is also **Yerushalayim** (Israeli) and **al-Quads ash-sharif** (Muslim).
• **Jaffa** is also **Joppa** and **Yafo**.
• **Eilat** is also **Elath** and **Elat**.
• **Acre** may appear as **Acco** and **Akko**.
• **Lake Tiberias** is the same as **Lake Kinneret** (Israeli) and the **Sea of Galilee** (Christian).

▼ *Below: Much of what you'll see in the Jerusalem Archaeological Park dates back to the Second Temple Period.*

and some ancient tombs. There's a breathtaking view of the **Temple Mount** through one of the windows. Open 08:00–12:00 and 14:30–17:00 daily.

Jerusalem Archaeological Park ★★

The Jerusalem Archaeological Park is an archaeological dig and open-air museum stretching from the **Temple Mount** in the north, the slope of the **Mount of Olives** and the **Kidron Valley** in the east and the **Valley of Hinnom** to the west and the south. Much of what you can see dates back to the Second Temple Period; at one point, there is a pile of huge stones, fallen from the Western Wall, and a direct result of the destruction of the Second Temple. There is also a staircase located south of the Temple Mount, leading to the **Double (Hulda) Gate**, and a series of stone-cut channels connecting the area with the Temple Mount. Ritual baths (miqva'ot) and cisterns were uncovered throughout the area as well as a **Herodian street**.

Also located in the archaeological park is the **Davidson Centre**, an audio-visual display in an underground storage complex, excavated only in 2001, belonging to an Umayyad Palace from the 7th century AD. Visitors can see a fascinating audiovisual reconstruction of the **Herodian Temple Mount** in AD 70, prior to the destruction of the Second Temple by the Romans. Open Sun–Thu 08:00–17:00, Fri 08:00–14:00.

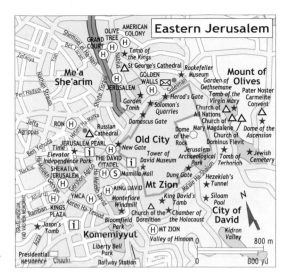

City of David ★★

Outside the Dung Gate of the Old City is a fascinating archaeological dig, now a major visitor attraction, slowly uncovering the City of David on and under the slopes of the Kidron Valley.

The excavation of the City of David is uncovering secrets from more than 3000 years ago, when King David left the city of Hebron for a small hilltop settlement known as Jerusalem, establishing it as the unified capital of the tribes of Israel. The City of David extended down the hill southwards from what is now **Temple Mount**. Its location was of strategic importance, surrounded by valleys on three sides, providing natural protection, and on top of the **Gihon Spring**, one of the biggest water sources in the Judean mountains and later to become the main water source for Jerusalem for over 1000 years.

This is a fascinating visit for all ages. Much of the interactive one-hour tour is underground, visiting some of the newest archaeological excavations at the site – fortresses and tunnels buried beneath millennia of history.

DOUBTS RAISED ON HEZEKIAH'S TUNNEL

During new excavations in 2011, archaeologists Ronny Reich of the University of Haifa and Eli Shukron of the Israel Antiquities Authority challenged the dates originally put forward for Hezekiah's Tunnel. They suggested that it originated in thelate 9th or early 10th century BC. Two more archaeologists support this theory as a result of pottery analysis.

BARS AND CAFÉS

Jerusalem has plenty of lively places in which to spend the evening. The bars along Ben Yehuda Street and the cluster of side streets around it are always busy, while the German Colony has several excellent café-bars, good for lunch or dinner. The ultra-fashionable Mamilla Mall, just outside the Old City, also has some stunning views of the city walls at night. On a Saturday morning, head for the leafy suburb of Ein Karem, where there are two or three excellent lunch spots.

You'll see the impressive shaft discovered in 1867 by the archaeologist **Charles Warren**, through which the people of the city drew water from the spring. The underground part of the tour ends at the Gihon Spring where, according to the Book of Kings in the Bible, Solomon was anointed king.

Part of the site is **Hezekiah's Tunnel**, an optional extension to the tour. In 701BC, Hezekiah, King of Judah, designed an ingenious tunnel connecting the Gihon Spring, the city's only water supply outside the city, to within the walls, creating the Siloam Pool to avoid having the water source cut off by the enemy. Workmen dug from both ends, zigzagging under the city until they met in the middle.

Today the 500m (550yd) Hezekiah's Tunnel is a highlight for many visitors who can trudge through the wet tunnel, holding a torch, a walk that take approximately 40 minutes. Ancient meets modern in the **Segway Tour**, using 'human transporters' (two-wheeled, gyroscopically controlled devices) to drive along some of the promenades overlooking Jerusalem. City of David open 08:00–19:00 Sun–Thu; 3D movie and sound and light show 19:00 and 21:00 Thu. Finally, an atmospheric night-time tour includes a 3D movie on the City of David's historic past and an impressive sound and light show which makes use of the ancient walls and architectural features.

MOUNT ZION ★★

Mount Zion, a rounded hillock outside the **Zion Gate**, appears as something rather more substantial in the Bible. It was here that the Virgin Mary is said to have died, a spot now marked by the **Church of the Dormition**. Jesus is also said to have washed the disciples' feet here before the **Last Supper**.

Symbolic with the promise of a Jewish homeland, Mount Zion has also been the subject of political tussles over the years. Suleiman is supposed to have executed the architect who designed the city walls here for failing to include Mount Zion in what was then Jerusalem.

There is a Catholic cemetery here in which **Oskar Schindler** is buried. Schindler saved the lives of 1200 Jews during the Holocaust and his story was later made into an award-winning movie, *Schindler's List*.

The Garden Tomb ✶

Anglicans believe that the 'real' Golgotha lies outside the current city walls. The Garden Tomb, through the Damascus Gate, does match the biblical description. The hill beside it is shaped like a skull and the rock-hewn cavern is typical of the time. The tomb was discovered in 1883 by General Charles Gordon.

Today, it is maintained by the British Garden Tomb Association, the entrance overlooking an English country garden. Open 08:30–17:30 daily.

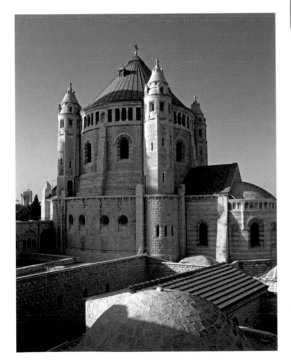

◀ *Left: The Church of the Dormition on Mount Zion commemorates the spot where the Virgin Mary is said to have died.*

JERUSALEM

▲ *Above: Among the city's plushest hotels is the King David.*

Rockefeller Museum ★★

Near the Garden Tomb, the Rockefeller Museum houses an interesting display of archaeological finds, including human bones from the Carmel area, dating back some 100,000 years and, recently, an exhibition of historical black-and-white photographs. Opening hours are 10:00–15:00 Sun–Thu, (excl. Tue) 10:00–14:00 Sat.

WEST JERUSALEM

The 'new' Jerusalem is a lively modern city, surprisingly green with tall cypress and shady pine trees. The shops and restaurants of **Zion Square** are a good place to get your bearings. Just off the square, **Ben Yehuda** and **Yoel Salomon** streets are pretty pedestrianized areas with plenty of art and craft shops.

King David Hotel ★

Located on Ha-Melekh David Street, this hotel is a Jerusalem landmark. The British used it as a base during the Mandate Period and a whole wing was blown up in July 1946 by the Jewish Underground, who hid bombs in milk churns. Bomb warnings were ignored and 91 people died, leading for calls for the British to withdraw from Israel. This event did not deter modern heads of state, all of whom stay here today.

Opposite the King David Hotel, the **YMCA** is another celebrated building. It was designed in 1928–33 by architects Shreve, Lamb and Harmon, who were also responsible for the Empire State Building in New York City. Not unlike the graceful minaret of a mosque, the 35m (120ft) tower offers stunning views of the city.

Time Elevator *

The Time Elevator at 37 Hillel Street is a great cheat's guide to the history of Jerusalem, narrating 3000 years of drama, from the City of David to the 1967 Six Day War. Moving seats, surround sound and special effects guarantee you'll feel part of history itself. It is open Sun–Thu 10:00–17:00, Fri 10:00–14:00 and Sat 12:00–18:00.

Yemin Moshe **

The most desirable address in Jerusalem today is the suburb of Yemin Moshe, overlooking the Old City and topped by a stone windmill. Its pretty stone buildings were the homes of the first Jewish colony to settle outside the safety of the city walls.

The patron of the colony, the English-Jewish philanthropist **Sir Moses Montefiore**, visited Jerusalem in 1858 and was so appalled by the cramped conditions within the walls of the city that he decided to sponsor a new suburb. He enlisted wealthy New Orleans Jew, **Judah Touro**, to help with the ambitious project.

The new town was called **Mishkenot Sha'ananim**, or 'peaceful dwellings', and later renamed **Yemin Moshe**. It was badly damaged in the 1967 war but was rebuilt and soon established itself as a fashionable, artistic neighbourhood. The windmill at the highest point was built to grind flour for the colony. In 1948 it served as an important observation post for the Israeli army. Today the windmill holds Montefiore's horse-drawn carriage among other artefacts. Open 09:00–16:00 Sun–Thu, 09:00–13:00 Fri.

▼ *Below: The striking YMCA building, a city landmark.*

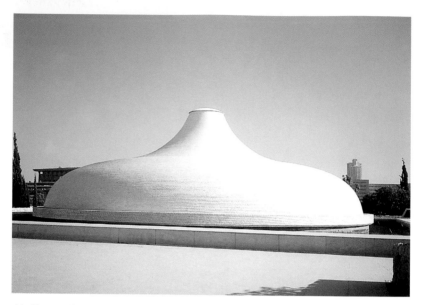

▲▶ Above and opposite: The Shrine of the Book resembles the lid of pots that contained the Dead Sea Scrolls.

Me'a She'arim ★

A few blocks north of Zion Square is the district of **Me'a She'arim**, built in 1875 as a refuge for the ultra-Orthodox Jews and, some might say, still resembling an old, East European-style ghetto. Walking through the narrow streets is like stepping back in time; old synagogues and grey buildings line the narrow streets, and the devout male residents, all pale-faced and bespectacled, sport black hats, long black robes and long, curly sidelocks of hair. Visitors are welcome but respectful dress and behaviour must be taken very seriously.

Israel Museum ★★★

The spectacular Israel Museum is an essential stop on a tour of Jerusalem. The museum covers art, archaeology, ethnology and its highlight, the **Dead Sea Scrolls**. You can't miss it from a distance, as the Shrine of the Book is a curious peaked dome shape, resembling the stone casket in which the original scrolls were stored.

Start with the amazing scale model of Jerusalem in the Second Temple Period, from 516 BC. A guide is very helpful here, although you can rent audio guides from the visitor centre. Next, there's a film about the mysterious sect who lived at Qumran, the barren place near the Dead Sea where the scrolls were found.

The highlight, however, is the **Shrine of the Book**, at the centre of which is displayed the **Book of Isaiah**, the oldest biblical document known to man. The scrolls themselves, fragile scraps of parchment beautifully laid out under glass, are awe-inspiring. Many others, of course, are safely stored in archives.

To understand more about the times of the Old Testament, you should visit the breathtaking archaeological section where 6000-year-old pottery figures, Caananite sarcophagi and 4000-year-old metalwork are housed, alongside tomb inscriptions dating from the time of Jesus. The art sections are equally well laid out, if less dramatic, with sections of Jewish art, some good Impressionist work including Renoirs and Van Goghs, and outside, the attractive **Billy Rose Sculpture Gardens**. Wild herbs grow amongst the orderly flower beds and sculptures and there are magnificent views of the city. Open 10:00–17:00 Sun, Mon, Wed, Thu and Sat, 16:00–21:00 Tue and 10:00–14:00 Fri.

SAMSON'S BETRAYAL

Old Testament hero Samson was endowed by God with supernatural strength, provided no razor touched his long locks. Samson performed several great feats, including the strangling of a lion and the slaying of 1000 Philistines with the jaw bone of an ass. Then he was betrayed by his Philistine lover, Delilah, who had his head shaved and thereafter handed him over to the Philistine people. He was blinded and made a slave. But according to the Book of Judges, when Samson's hair grew back, he was once again able to exert his great strength at a Philistine festival where he was being paraded. He pulled down the pillars of the house in which 3000 people had assembled, burying the mob and himself in the ruins.

Yad Vashem Memorial ★★★

Some distance further west on Mount Herzl is the poignant Holocaust Memorial, dedicated to the six million Jews who were murdered by the Nazis. The main exhibit, the **Holocaust History Museum**, is a masterful piece of design in the shape of a triangular prism. You enter at one end and emerge at the other – there is no way out in between. The prism descends below ground level, emerging again into the light, the long glass strip in the ceiling illuminating the darkness below at its deepest point. Off the prism are different rooms with exhibitions telling the story, a mixture of harrowing film of the ghettos, awful statistics, artefacts, personal testimonies, memorabilia and multimedia

▲ *Above: Poignant sculpture at the Yad Vashem memorial.*

montages. At one point, there's a cutaway cattle train carriage.

The prism emerges back into sunlight at the end, with an uninterrupted view across forested hills. But this is only a fraction of Yad Vashem. Visit the **Hall of Names**, a dome-shaped structure with hundreds of thousands of images of people who were murdered by the Nazis gazing down from the ceiling. The top of the dome is open to the elements and below is a dark pool, reflecting the faces above, a symbol that they won't be forgotten. It is open 09:00–17:00 Sun–Wed, 09:00–20:00 Thu, 09:00–14:00 Fri.

THE WEST BANK

The largest area of the Occupied Palestinian Territories, the West Bank is one of Israel's most 'biblical' landscapes: low, rolling hills dotted with dusty olive trees, grazing donkeys and goats, rocky terraces, Bedouin encampments, and grubby children playing in the dust. From the hills outside Jerusalem, it is easy to spot the distant blue, metallic glint of the **Dead Sea**. But this is one of the most politically tense areas of the Middle East and the landscape in the 21st century is scarred by the Israeli 'Separation Barrier', hundreds of miles of concrete wall and fencing partitioning off the areas under the control of the **Palestinian Authority**, ostensibly to 'protect' Israel from terrorist incursions.

'West Bank' actually refers to the bank of the **River Jordan**, which divides Israel from its neighbour. Jordan annexed the region in 1950 and Israel subsequently gained control of it in 1967 during the Six Day War. The area is important for Israel; without this strip of land, there would be just 15km (9 1/2 miles) between Jordan and the Mediterranean in places, making Israeli territory dangerously thin. Several areas in the West Bank are now under the control of the Palestinian Authority, among them the towns of Nablus, Ramallah, Tulkarm, Jenin, Bethlehem and Jericho.

Many fascinating biblical sights are located on the West Bank, although whether travel to them is recommended depends entirely on the security situation at the time. **Bethlehem**, birthplace of Jesus, and **Jericho**, the oldest city known to man, are popular. Southeast of Bethlehem is **Herodian**, King Herod's magnificent desert citadel, and the grand monastery of **Mar Saba**. North of Jerusalem are several spots of biblical significance — **Beit El**, where Jacob dreamed of a ladder ascending to Heaven, and **Shiloh**, where the Ark of the Covenant was once housed.

WEST BANK DO'S AND DON'TS

- Do check the political climate before visiting the West Bank.
- Do dress modestly.
- Do dress like a tourist, for once! If you don't look Arabic or Israeli, you should be left alone.
- Do travel on a tour bus, less likely to be a target for kidnapping.
- Don't take a car with Israeli plates into the Palestinian-controlled cities. Use the bypass instead.
- Don't expect to spend the night.
- Do talk to the Palestinians; they're friendly and hospitable.

JERUSALEM

▶ *Right: Although other details of his life are occasionally subject to dispute, it is agreed that Jesus was born in Bethlehem; the Church of the Nativity has long been an essential religious site.*

JOSEPH, INTERPRETER OF DREAMS

Favourite son of Jacob, Joseph was envied by his 11 brothers, who sold him as a slave to a pharoah. Joseph, however, could interpret dreams and won the favour of the pharaoh by prophesying seven years of feast followed by seven years of famine. The pharaoh made Joseph his highest official and charged him with collecting food to be used during the years of famine. When the famine arrived, the Egyptians were able to survive as a result. The brothers came to Egypt, begging for food, and the family was reconciled.

BETHLEHEM

Bethlehem is only 11km (7 miles) south of Jerusalem but the difference in scenery is vivid as the little town is somewhat run-down and crumbling. Bethlehem is nonetheless a religious hotspot and, to many visitors, the Church of the Nativity is as essential a site as the Holy Sepulchre is in the city of Jerusalem. Try to spend at least half a day here rather than just visiting the main attractions; it's fascinating to wander through the narrow streets and there are some excellent falafel restaurants, too.

Church of the Nativity ★★

A solid-looking structure on Manger Square (today a parking

lot surrounded by cheap souvenir stalls), the Church of the Nativity, or at least its original basilica, has stood here since AD 325, and was built by the Emperor Constantine. Emperor Justinian later rebuilt it in the 6th century. Like the Church of the Holy Sepulchre in Jerusalem, the Church of the Nativity is too important a spot for only one denomination to occupy and there are Greek Orthodox, Armenian and Franciscan sections in this place of worship.

The door, which was bricked up by the Crusaders to stop their enemies from charging in on horseback, is so low that you have to stoop to get in. In the sombre gloom, gold-coloured lamps hang from the thick wooden ceiling and parts of the wooden floor gape open, revealing the old mosaics underneath.

The tiny **Grotto of the Nativity** is down some rather dark stone steps, a faded mosaic on the altar and a silver star on the floor marking the spot where Jesus is believed to have been born. At times, the grotto can get very crowded. Next door, the **Chapel of the Manger** is where Mary placed the baby Jesus in a manger – the reality, experts agree, is that Jesus was born not in a stable but in a cave or grotto similar to this; many houses in Bethlehem are still built backing onto the hill, which is riddled with caves. The actual manger is now kept in Rome in the Church of Santa Maria Maggiore. Open 06:00–18:00 daily (summer).

Milk Grotto ★

Along Milk Grotto Street, which leads off Manger Square, is a limestone cave of important religious significance. Legend has it that while Mary and Joseph were preparing to flee Bethlehem, some of Mary's milk splashed on the floor as she was nursing the baby, whitening the red rock.

Nowadays both Christians and Muslims believe that a visit to the cave will increase fertility and promote better breast-feeding. Visitors have been chipping away at the white stone for years. Little packets are sold by the souvenir vendors. Opening hours are 08:00–18:00 (summer), 08:00–17:00 (winter).

THE SEPARATION BARRIER

Israel's controversial Separation Barrier, known as the Apartheid Wall by the Palestinians, brutally cuts the landscape in half, slicing towns and individual streets in two. The wall, initially planned to extend for some 690km (429 miles) – although estimates vary greatly – is still under construction. To date, over 60% has already been built. Global organizations such as Amnesty International believe that the construction violates human rights as it cuts farmers from their land, residents of villages from their relatives, and individual Palestinians from their places of work, from health-care facilities and from schools.

ISRAEL'S AREA CODES

Israel's area dialling codes are as follows:
02 – Jerusalem
03 – Tel Aviv
04 – Haifa, Galilee and the north
07 – The south including Eilat and Be'er Sheva
08 – Ashdod
09 – Herzliya and Netanya

▲ *Above: A silver star marks the spot where Jesus is believed to have been born.*

The Shepherds' Fields ★

A visit to Bethlehem would not be complete without seeing the fields where shepherds watched their flocks and saw the angels proclaiming the birth of Christ. Go by taxi or walk the short distance along the imaginatively named Shepherd's Street off Manger Square to the Arab village of **Beit Salur**. Two churches mark the spot where the shepherds were supposedly sitting: a **Greek church** stands in the field, while the **Franciscan Church of the Angels** covers the caves where the shepherds lived.

King David's Well ★

Also in Bethlehem is David's Well, consisting of three rock-hewn water cisterns, situated on Manger Street opposite the King David Cinema. During a battle with the Philistines, King David sent three of his men to break through the Philistine ranks to fetch water. But when they returned, the king sacrificed the water to God, rather than 'drink the blood of the men who went at the risk of their lives'.

BEST TIMES TO VISIT

March to May and late September to October are the best times to visit as the heat is not too oppressive during these times. Winter in Jerusalem can be damp, grey and chilly (or on the other hand dazzlingly clear), so take warm clothes for November to February. Midsummer can be very hot, which makes sightseeing more difficult. **September** is the main Jewish holiday period, so check the calendar before planning a trip as many of the attractions will be closed at this time.

GETTING THERE

The closest airport to Jerusalem is Tel Aviv's Ben Gurion International airport, about 40 minutes from the city by **taxi** or **sherut**: try Nesher Tours, tel: 02 625 7227. There are regular Egged **bus** services from Tel Aviv (www.egged.co.il) and other parts of the country, as well as **trains** from Tel Aviv (www.rail.co.il). You can rent a **car** at Ben Gurion but there is little point if your only destination is Jerusalem, as traffic is bad in the city, not to mention parking. Public transport or walking are much better ways to get around.

To get to Bethlehem other than on a booked tour, you have to take either an Arab bus (no. 21) or a private *sherut* taxi from the Damascus Gate (Bab el-Amoud) in East Jerusalem via Beit Jala to Bethlehem. There is an Israeli check-point on the road to Bethlehem which may cause delays. You must carry a passport. Israelis cannot enter the West Bank so any tour will pick up a Palestinian guide once through the checkpoint. Tours and *sheruts* may be held up by the need to change vehicles at the checkpoint; everything depends on the security situation at the time.

GETTING AROUND

The only real way to get around the largely pedestrianized Old City is on foot, through the narrow alleyways and up and down many steps. There are plenty of guided tours for every possible interest (Christian or Jewish, for example), or you can get a map from the tourist information office at the Jaffa Gate and find your own way around. If you are in a wheelchair or have trouble walking, visit the excellent website www.accessinisrael.org which has planned out step-free routes around the Old City and also includes useful information about accessible areas inside the main attractions.

WHERE TO STAY

Jerusalem offers visitors the complete range of accommodation, from five-star de-luxe hotels to simple hostels, youth hostels, Christian or Jewish hostels and even a kibbutz within the city limits. Most of the hotels have kosher restaurants.

Luxury

Dan Boutique Hotel, 31 Hebron Road, tel: 02 568 9999, www.danhotels.com Petite version of the bigger Dan Hotels, with rooftop gym, chic bar, amazing views of the Old City and Mount Zion. It is also close to Yemin Moshe and the German Colony.

American Colony Hotel, 1 Louis Vincent Street, Jerusalem, tel: 02 627 9777, www.americancolony.com Romantic and legendary, with colourful history. Popular with visiting diplomats. Gorgeous décor, cocktail bar, pool, three restaurants.

Olive Tree Hotel, 23 St George St, tel: 02 541 0410, www.olivetreehotel.com Large and luxurious new hotel with architectural touches reflecting the Old City and an olive tree in the atrium. Restaurant, indoor pool, bar.

The King David Hotel, 23 King David Street, tel: 02 620 8888, www.danhotels.com

Luxurious flagship of the Dan Hotels chain, favoured by VIPs and offering beautiful views of the Old City.

The David Citadel Hotel, 7 King David Street, tel: 02 621 1111, www.thedavidcitadel.com Luxury five-star hotel facing the Old City. Family-friendly, with heated pool.

Mid-range

Austrian Hospice of the Holy Family, Via Dolorosa 37, Old City, Jerusalem, tel: 02 626 5800, www.austrianhospice. com Simple but comfortable rooms with private facilities as well as dormitories. Located in the heart of the Old City. Has an Austrian café – quite incongruous – serving excellent *sacher torte* with whipped cream, apple strudel, goulash soup and Wiener schnitzel with potato salad.

Jerusalem Hotel, Nablus Road, tel: 02 628 3282, www.jrshotel.com Beautifully decorated, family-run hotel in old Arab mansion with garden patio designed to simulate a Palestinian village. It is popular with media and creative types. The hotel offers tours to Palestinian areas as well as political tours of Jerusalem.

Eldan Hotel, 24 King David St, tel: 02 567 9777, www.eldanhotel.com

Hotel is centrally located. **Grand Court**, 15 St George Street, tel: 02 591 7777, www.grandhotels-israel.com Big hotel with rooftop pool and restaurant; within walking distance of the Damascus Gate.

Mount Zion, 17 Hebron Road, Jerusalem, tel: 02 568 9555, www.mountzion.co.il Landmark hotel in lush gardens near the Old City. Stunning views from the lounge bar.

Budget

Agron Guest House, Agron 6, tel: 02 594 5522, www.iyha.org.il This establishment has 55 rooms and two restaurants. It is within walking distance of the sights of the Old City.

Mount of Olives Hotel, 53 Mount of Olives Rd, tel: 02 628 4877, www.mtolives.com Friendly, family-run hotel right next to the Church of the Ascension, with a fun bar under what resembles a Bedouin tent. It affords stunning views of the Old City.

Abraham Hostel, 67 Ha Nevi'im St, tel: 02 650 2200, www.abrahamhostels.com This is a relatively new hostel chain but already highly rated, located a short walk from central Jerusalem and the Old City.

Where to Eat

Jerusalem is a great city for coffee bars and street dining, from the Arab stalls in the Old City to the pavement cafés along Ben Yehuda. Explore everything from Middle Eastern specialities (known as Oriental) to French gourmet, Italian and Asian.

Luxury

American Colony Hotel, Nablus Road, tel: 02 627 9777. Quiet, elegant surroundings. Barbecues are held in the garden on Saturdays in summer.

Rooftop Restaurant, 11 King Solomon St, tel: 02 548 2230. Above Mamilla Hotel, highly rated, great views.

Mid-range

Blue Dolphin, 7 Shimon Hazadik St, tel: 02 532 2001. Excellent fish restaurant, serving ocean fish and St Peter's fish from Galilee as well as Lebanese specialities and excellent salads.

Montefiore, Under the Windmill, Yemin Moshe, tel: 053 809 4733, www.2eat. co.il/eng/montefiore Kosher dairy with wonderful cheesy pasta, huge salads and decadent desserts.

Le Tsriff, YMCA Hotel, 5 Horkanus St, tel: 02 624 2478. Terrace dining at the spectacular YMCA building. French and vegetarian food, huge baked pies.

Budget
Abu Shukri,
63 El Wad Road, tel: 02 627 1538. This is one of the old city's most famous falafel joints, very basic, selling falafel in pitas, dollops of hummus, beans and salads, perfect for a quick lunch on the run.

SHOPPING
Much of the Old City is taken up with market stalls, particularly in the Muslim quarter, where you'll find a wide range of souvenirs, including olivewood chess and nativity sets, rosaries, wooden camels, glassware from Hebron, mother-of-pearl objects, lovely silver jewellery and leather goods. You will also see Bedouin weavings and rugs of varying quality. There are further stalls selling spices, oils, potions, sticky baklava cakes and fake designer bags, suitcases and designer clothes. Haggle hard for everything. Some of the nicer shops sell tasteful (and comical) Judaica, from menorahs to Western Wall fridge magnets.
The shops along the **Cardo** are more glitzy, and here you'll find expensive designer jewellery and high-class Judaica as well as antiques and art galleries. For designer clothing, don't miss the Mamilla Mall at the end of Jaffa Road.

TOURS AND EXCURSIONS
Jerusalem is one city where visitors really will benefit from the knowledge and experience of a guide, at the very least for a walking tour around the Old City.
The **Municipality of Jerusalem** offers a free walking tour with a qualified guide on Sat only, tel: 02 629 5363. For details, visit www.jerusalem.mun.il
Other free tours (2 hours) of the Old City are offered by Sandemans New Europe Jerusalem three times a day from Jaffa Gate, visiting all the historic sites including the four Old City quarters, plus views of the Western Wall and over the city. Guides rely on tips alone, although there is no pressure to give them. Visit www.newjerusalemtours.com
Guided tours are offered by numerous operators. Try **Jerusalem Experience**, tel: 077 558 6001, www.jerusalemexperience.co.il for small group tours (up to six) with different themes – Jewish, Three Religions, King David, for example. Or book a private tour guide; all guides

registered with the tourist board are listed, with the languages they speak, on www.goisrael.com before you go.
Abu Hassan Alternative Tours operates half- and full-day tours to Palestinian towns and villages; tel: 052 286 4205, www.alternativetours.ps
Bein Harim also offers various combinations including Bethlehem; tel: 03 542 2000, www.beinharim.tours.com
For tours through the **Western Wall Tunnels**, you have to book in advance; tel: 02 627 1333, www.thekotel.org
Tourist Information Centre, Jaffa Gate, tel: 02 627 1422. Information on **Bethlehem**: Open Bethlehem, www.openbethlehem.org Excellent site dedicated to the preservation of the Holy City and its religious heritage.
Police Emergency No., tel: 100.
Lost Credit Card Lines, Amex, tel: 03 636 4445; MC, tel: 180 941 8873.
Christian Information Centre, Jaffa Gate, Jerusalem 91142, tel: 02 627 2692. For religious places of interest, visit www.cicts.org

JERUSALEM	J	F	M	A	M	J	J	A	S	O	N	D
AVERAGE TEMP. °F	48	48	55	61	68	73	75	77	73	70	61	52
AVERAGE TEMP. °C	9	9	13	16	20	23	24	25	23	21	16	11
RAINFALL in	5.2	5.2	2.5	1.1	0.1	0	0	0	0	.51	2.8	3.4
RAINFALL mm	132	132	64	28	3	0	0	0	0	13	71	86
Days of rainfall	9	8	7	3	1	0	0	0	0	1	5	8

3
Tel Aviv

Greater Tel Aviv is home to some 2.4 million people, the core city to a surprisingly low 415,000. Just 105 years old, Tel Aviv's eclectic architectural style reflects the many new waves of immigrants: their dreams of recreating the neoclassical grace of Vienna, ornate experimentation with Art Nouveau and the minimalist lines of Bauhaus style. In amongst this unlikely collection of buildings, the traffic roars, the cafés buzz with conversation and the working population goes about its frenetic daily business. After work and at weekends everybody heads for the city's beaches, to swim, sunbathe or simply stroll along the promenade.

Any visitor thirsting for a bit of history can venture slightly south to Jaffa, one of the world's oldest cities steeped in biblical tales and mythology. A colourful artistic community thrives here today. In addition, **Jaffa** offers a fine line in nightlife, with lively bars and clubs open well into the small hours.

To the north of the Tel Aviv–Jaffa area, along the sweeping expanse of the Mediterranean beaches, is Israel's exclusive resort of **Herzliya**, haunt of the rich and beautiful, as well as **Netanya**, heart of the country's important diamond-cutting industry. Southwest is **Rishon le-Zion**, set amongst rolling vineyards, and **Ashkelon**, birthplace of Herod the Great.

Tel Aviv also makes a convenient base for exploring the rest of the country; Israel's main international airport, Ben Gurion, is located nearby, while Jerusalem, for example, is only 30 minutes along the motorway.

DON'T MISS

*** Jaffa: visit the world's oldest working harbour which has great views of the bay.
*** Beth Hatefutsoth Museum: tells the story of the Diaspora.
** Carmel Market: experience the hustle and bustle of the market.
** National Antiquities Park: explore magnificent ruins at Ashkelon.
** Rishon le-Zion: taste wonderful wines.
* Netanya: window-shop for diamonds.

◄ *Opposite: Extensive sandy beaches line modern Tel Aviv.*

TEL AVIV

TEL AVIV

Tel Aviv is actually the first Jewish city to have been built in 2000 years. In 1909, a group of families from the rather over-crowded, predominantly Arab port of Jaffa staked their claim on the sand dunes to the north. The new suburb which they created – named Tel Aviv, or Hill of Spring – expanded rapidly until, in 1948, it became the capital of Israel (the Israelis see Jerusalem as their capital but this status is not recognized by the international community as Jerusalem is still disputed territory with the Palestinians). Today, big hotels tower over Tel Aviv's beaches, while Shenken Street and the surround-

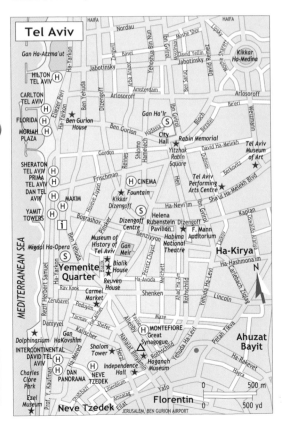

ing area is a high-profile and elegant fashion district and Lilienblum Street, the hip suburb of Neve Tzedek and, increasingly, Florentin offer nightlife to rival any European capital.

Yemenite Quarter *

In the shadow of the Shalom Tower lies the bustling Yemenite Quarter, which hasn't changed much over the last 100 years. Low-rise stone houses line the noisy, narrow streets, all with a distinctly Arabic flavour. Some of the best Middle Eastern restaurants in the city are located here, specializing in pungent Yemenite cuisine.

Carmel Market **

Close by, around Ha-Carmel Street, is the colourful Carmel Street Market, a riot of sights, sounds and smells. Fragrant herbs, juicy piles of fruits, sumptuous green vegetables and more exotic specimens like yellow star fruit and piles of glistening dates are all on sale alongside clothes and kitchenware, and the aromas of freshly baked pitta and the ubiquitous fried falafel wafting by.

Nahalat Binyamin **

Every Tuesday and Friday, there's an arts and crafts market in a couple of pedestrianized streets near **Carmel Market**. This is a great place to browse the stalls for handmade jewellery,

▲ *Above: Carmel Market is a medley of colours, sights and smells.*
▼ *Below left: Tel Aviv seen from the Shalom Tower.*

TEL AVIV

▶ *Right: Dizengoff Circle, a focal point of Tel Aviv.*

Judaica with a contemporary twist (amusing clocks, fridge magnets and so on), wood-carved items, scented candles and soaps, plants, pots and paintings, including a couple of places selling beautiful black-and-white photographic prints of Israel. Get there early as it gets very busy. The street is lined with cafés for breakfast (the market is open around 10:00–17:00, Tue and Fri, longer hours in summer).

The White City ★★★

Tel Aviv is home to the world's largest collection of buildings constructed in the **Bauhaus** style, a UNESCO-protected area known as the **White City**. The area is bordered by Allenby Street in the south, Begin Road in the east, the Yarkon River to the north and the Mediterranean to the west, although in reality, most of the finest examples are along **Rothschild Boulevard**.

More than 4000 properties were built in the Bauhaus style. The city's layout was actually planned by a Scotsman, **Sir Patrick Geddes**, but individual buildings were designed by Jewish architects who had studied in Europe before returning to Palestine in the 1920s to live in the growing Tel

Aviv, and then in the 1930s, fleeing the rise of Nazi Germany.

Between 1500 and 2000 buildings in Tel Aviv have been protected as part of the world's greatest concentration of Bauhaus structures. Some of the buildings are obvious, with their gleaming, restored façades and clean, minimalist lines. Others have not been touched in a century and are crumbling, with scruffy gardens and broken panes of glass.

The architectural style of Bauhaus and its close relatives is characterized by asymmetry, simplicity and functionality, with solid balconies, flat roofs and, in the stairwells, narrow windows that curiously resemble the glass on a thermometer, stacked on top of one another. On first sight, the buildings appear stark, but if you look closely, many have exquisite details – graceful pillars, the use of glass bricks to allow light in, simple motifs reflecting the architect's individual passions, – although the style does not permit any unnecessary adornment.

Dizengoff Circle Area ★★★

If you're intrigued by the Bauhaus movement, call in at the **Bauhaus Center** at 99 Dizengoff Street for information about the movement as well as paintings, furniture for sale, miniatures and photography.

Dizengoff Circle is a raised piazza with an unusual fountain at its centre – a series of coloured, cog-like rings which rotate. Every hour, on the hour, there's a musical display with jets of water and a flame.

A few streets to the south is the **Dizengoff Centre**, a busy shopping centre with restaurants and cinemas.

Shenken Street ★★

Shenken has long since taken over from Dizengoff as the coolest fashion street in the city, lined on both sides with designer shops; not haute couture, but young, fashionable Israeli labels like **Ronen Chen**, whose fluid dresses and separates are perfect for the working woman, and **Naama Bezalel**, for unique, super-chic fashion designs. **Michal Negrin** sells vintage-inspired jewellery and accessories, as

---

GOLDEN SANDS

Tel Aviv's coast can have strong **undercurrents**, so never swim when the black flag is flying and be careful if the red one is raised. Watch your valuables; while violent crime is uncommon in Israel, there's plenty of petty theft. Many of the beaches have deck chairs and lockers to rent. Beware, however, of flying objects! Paddleball, or *matzkot*, is a national passion. Players have round wooden bats and hit the ball back and forth, making frequent enthusiastic dives into the sand.

Citrus fruit is Israel's most valuable agricultural export, yet is not indigenous to the country. The coastal strip, which now presents ideal growing conditions, was until 150 years ago a malaria-infested swamp. It was the hardy pioneers in the last century who installed pumps to drain the swamps and pump up fresh water for the fledgling orchards. Jaffa eventually became the most important port for citrus, hence the name **Jaffa Oranges**, and today, acres of scented orange, lemon and grapefruit groves line the coast.

well as pretty items for the home, while **Sabon** is the place to call at for scented candles and soaps. There are sports shops, grungy teenage fashions, tattoo parlours and book-shops, too – in effect, everything.

Shenken is right next to a very picturesque, tree-lined, up-and-coming residential neighbourhood, the inhabitants of which emerge on Saturday mornings for breakfast and coffee in the many street cafés.

Gan Ha-Hashmal *

Tel Aviv is a cutting-edge centre for young, talented designers and you can find their ateliers dotted around the city. You have to know where they are, though, as many are tucked away in small, unassuming neighbourhoods, unable to afford the high rents in trendy places like Neve Tzedek.

Gan Ha-Hashmal, or the **Electric Garden**, to the east of the southern end of Rothschild, is such an area, recently gentrified, with a scruffy little park at its centre. In the streets around here are such treasures as **Kisim** whose gorgeous leather bags were featured in the 2008 movie, Sex and the City. **Mira Mory** is a jewellery workshop that makes use of a unique knitting technique to produce deli-cate mesh-style gold and silver pieces. Designer Shani Bar uses geometric influences to create shoes that are a fusion of modern and classic styles.

Yitzhak Rabin Square **

Overlooked by the concrete block of the **City Hall**, Yitzhak Rabin Square has been named after the much-loved Israeli prime minister, an important architect of the Middle East peace process and winner of the Nobel Peace Prize. Rabin was killed on 4 November 1995 by three bullets fired by right-wing Israeli radical Yigal Amir, who was opposed to Rabin's signing of the Oslo Accords. The assassination took place at a packed rally in the square in support of the government's peace policy.

The bleak-looking monument to Rabin was erected a year

Why not take a sunset stroll along the beach to Jaffa? The old port is visible all the way along the wide, sandy strip and the walk is mar-vellously invigorating after a day's sightseeing in the heat. Once you arrive at Jaffa, simply climb over the hill to the main square, lined with bars and restaurants.

after his murder. Created by the sculptor **Yael Ben-Artzi**, the memorial is made of 16 basalt stones from the **Golan Heights**. Thousands gather here every year on the anniversary of Rabin's death – a sobering moment. The square is also, however, a symbol of Israel's desire for peace

Tel Aviv Museum of Art ★★

The wonderful Tel Aviv Museum of Art is housed in three buildings. The **Helena Rubenstein Pavilion** at the top of Rothschild Boulevard houses temporary exhibitions of contemporary art. Nearby there's the **Art Education Centre** and on Sha'ul Ha-Melekh Boulevard is the museum's **main site**, with permanent collections of Israeli and modern art and a large European section from the 16th to the 19th centuries.

For lovers of contemporary art, this place is a paradise and a breathtaking example of Israel's deep connections with serious collectors all over the world, many of whom have loaned pieces to the museum. There is work by Paul Cézanne, Alfred Sisley, Henri Edmond Cross, Pierre Bonnard, Henri Matisse, Amedeo Modigliani and Marc Chagall in the Simon and Marie Jaglom Collection, which focuses on French art of the turn of the 19th century, while the Moshe and Sara Mayer Collection features pieces by Degas, Renoir, Monet, Pissarro, Gauguin, Van Gogh, Cézanne, Miró and big names

ANDROMEDA'S ROCK

The Greek myth of Perseus and Andromeda comes from the old port of Jaffa. Legend has it that the king of Jaffa (in some indeterminate period of history) chained his beautiful daughter Andromeda to a rock outside the port to appease a particularly vicious sea monster. Perseus, on his winged white horse, snatched Andromeda from the jaws of death and bore her off into the sunset. Some 2000 years ago, residents of the port even believed that the chains that bound Andromeda and the skeleton of the monster were visible in the sea.

TEL AVIV

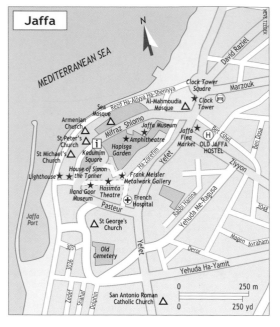

Jaffa

MEDITERRANEAN SEA

Armenian Church
Sea Mosque
St Peter's Church
St Michael's Church
Kedumim Square
Lighthouse
House of Simon the Tanner
Ilana Goor Museum
Hasimta Theatre
French Hospital
Jaffa Port
St George's Church
Old Cemetery
San Antonio Roman Catholic Church

Clock Tower Square
Al-Mahmoudia Mosque
Clock Tower
Marzouk
David Raziel
Jaffa Museum
Amphitheatre
Hapisga Garden
Jaffa Flea Market
OLD JAFFA HOSTEL
Frank Meisler Metalwork Gallery
Yehuda Me-Ragusa
Rabbi Hanina
Deror
Yehuda Ha-Yamit
Magen Avraham

0   250 m
0   250 yd

from various other genres including Cubism and German Expressionism. You'll find far more, though; allow at least half a day for a visit. Open 10:00–18:00 Mon, Wed, Sat; 10:00–21:00 Tue, Thu; 10:00–14:00 Fri; closed Sun.

The Tel Aviv Performing Arts Centre ★★★

Next to the main museum building (you can walk between the two buildings) is the graceful **Tel Aviv Performing Arts Centre (TAPAC)**, residence of the **Israeli Opera**. Designed by the late Ya'akov Rechter, it opened in 1994 and is the focal point for cultural and artistic events in Tel Aviv. The foyer is a futuristic, curvy space created by architect-designer **Ron Arad**. Everything is curved, from the stairs to the box office, the chairs, the wall of glass and the bar of the chic little café. There are temporary art exhibitions in the foyer, performances at the small amphitheatre and an impressive music shop. The foyer is open Sun–Thu 09:30–20:30 and Fri 09:30–13:00, as well as during performances (www.israel-opera.co.il).

Harry Oppenheimer Diamond Museum, Ramat Gan

This museum in Tel Aviv's Diamond Exchange tells the history of diamonds and displays models of some of the world's most famous stones, including the Koh-i-Noor diamond and the legendary stone given by Richard Burton to Elizabeth Taylor. Open 10:00–16:00 Sun, Mon, Thu, and 10:00–18:00 Tue.

Beaches *

Tel Aviv is unusual in that it has great beaches – for most of the time safe to swim from and pleasantly uncrowded – right on its doorstep. Broad, sandy and very clean, the beaches in front of the **Hilton** all the way south to the **Charles Clore Park** are patrolled by lifeguards. Windsurfing, sailing and jet skis are available for hire.

JAFFA

Unlike modern Tel Aviv, Jaffa's history stretches back thousands of years. Jaffa is Hebrew for 'beautiful', and was given to the port by Noah's youngest son, Japheth, who decided to settle here after the great Flood had subsided. The prophet **Jonah** fled to Tarshish from Jaffa, encountering a whale along the way, while cedars of Lebanon were once offloaded at this ancient harbour for the construction of Solomon's Temple in Jerusalem.

Jaffa thrived as a port for an astonishing 4000 years, being invaded, knocked down and rebuilt at least 15 times. Under British Mandate, however, Haifa became Israel's main port and Jaffa fell into decline. Following waves of invest-

▼ *Below: Jerusalem Beach is one of the most popular and a likely spot for an impromptu game of beach volleyball.*

ment on the part of the government, Jaffa today is beautifully preserved, its tangle of stone alleyways the haunt of artists and sculptors, its mainly Arab population living peacefully side by side with their brash, flashy, multicultural neighbour, modern Tel Aviv.

Exploring Jaffa on Foot ★★★

Old Jaffa is easy to explore on foot. By day, the streets are buzzing with tourists shopping for art and enjoying some of the city's most celebrated restaurants and patisseries (don't miss lunch on the hoof from **Abouelafia**, the famous 24-hour bakery on Yefet Street), as well as the famous flea market. Getting orientated is easy. Busy **Yefet Street** bisects the area; its start is marked by the **Clock Tower**. On its other side is the **Flea Market**.

Every week, the Association for Tourism Tel Aviv-Jaffa (www.visit-tel-aviv.com) offers four free English-guided tours for tourists, no advance reservation required: Art and architecture at Tel Aviv University (Mon 11:00); Old Jaffa (Wed 09:30 or 10:00); Tel Aviv by night (Tue 20:00); and Bauhaus "the White City" (Sat 11:00).

▼ *Below: Old Jaffa, a must for any visitor to Tel Aviv.*

Old Jaffa Visitors' Centre *

There's a small, subterranean visitors' centre at the entrance to the old town on **Kedumim Square**, mainly underground, showing relics from Jaffa's long history and an audiovisual presentation (in English and other languages) about the port's past. It is open 09:00–20:00 Sat–Thu, 09:00–17:00 Fri (winter). Longer hours in summer.

The Clock Tower *

The **Ottoman Clock Tower**, dating back to 1906, was built on Yefet Street in the Ottoman era to commemorate Sultan Abdul Hamid II's 25th year in power. The epicentre of Jaffa, the clock is the city's meeting place, as well as the start point for the free guided tours offered by the tourist association. A series of stained-glass windows around the tower tells the story of the town's history. Further along the road, past the police station, is the **Al-Mahmoudiya Mosque**, built in 1812 and named after the then Turkish governor. Non-Muslims are not allowed inside. Jaffa Museum is located in the former City Hall, which has also served as a post office, public bath and police station.

St Peter's Church *

This imposing church was built by Franciscan monks between 1888 and 1894. There has been a church on the site, close to where St Peter is said to have had a visitation from an angel, for centuries, once serving as a hostel for pilgrims on their way to Jerusalem. There was also a Crusader castle here. Down a narrow alley close by is the **House of Simon the Tanner**, who is mentioned in the Bible (Acts 10:9–42), and who was playing host to Peter at the time of the visitation. The house is inhabited today by an Armenian family and is not open to the public.

Ilana Goor Museum ***

This fascinating museum on Mazal Dagim Street in Old Jaffa is an example of living with art. A hostel for Jewish pilgrims in the 18th century, today it is the home of artist and sculptor

FUN-FILLED FIELD SCHOOLS

The Society for the Protection of Nature operates 26 field schools in Israel, each specializing in ecology and natural history. Many have simple accommodation for visitors, usually with shared bathroom and communal dining room, and make a great place to stay far from the beaten track. A wide variety of hikes and excursions, all of them educational, are run from the field schools, including mountain-trail walking and desert safaris.

TEL AVIV

▶ *Right: The fascinating Ilana Goor Museum in Old Jaffa, one of many art galleries to explore.*

Ilana Goor, who opens most of her personal living space to the public. There are spectacular sculptures, many using agricultural tools; whole rooms containing just one scene, often of strange metal birds and insects; and some beautiful paintings, as well as the artist's personal collection of paintings, carvings, castings and etchings from her travels worldwide. Open 10:00–16:00 Sun–Fri and 10:00–18:00 Sat.

Jaffa Flea Market ★★
The famous flea market is opposite Old Jaffa, across Yefet Street, from Sunday to Friday. It's a treasure-trove of junk (and the occasional find) spilling out of the buildings and warehouses, offering anything from oriental rugs to knock-off designer jeans. Open Sun–Thu, 09:00–17:00 (later in summer); Fri 09:00–14:00.

NIGHTLIFE

As well as **Jaffa**, with its seafood restaurants, bars and clubs, many of which stay open into the small hours, Tel Aviv has various other focal points for nightlife. Some of the smartest restaurants are in Neve Tzedek, one of the most desirable places to live, close to Lilienblum Street, the epicentre of cool lounge bars. Another hot ticket in Neve Tzedek is the new Tachana entertainment complex, occupying the site of the old historic railway station (1892).

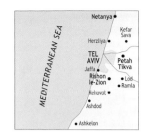

There are some wonderful restaurants to be found along the vast stretch of beach, too, mainly specializing in seafood, and there's a cluster of bars and huge nightclubs at the award-winning Tel Aviv Port, or New Port, at the northern end of the beach.

DAY TRIPS FROM TEL AVIV

Long, sandy beaches stretch in an unbroken line south from Tel Aviv to the Gaza Strip. The beaches near the towns can sometimes be busy, as Israelis take refuge from the summer humidity to indulge in sunbathing, windsurfing or swimming.

Rishon le-Zion ★★

Just a short drive southeast from Tel Aviv, Rishon le-Zion was one of the first new Jewish settlements in Israel. The name, which means 'First in Zion', was coined by a group of Russian and Polish Jews who arrived here in 1882, fleeing the pogroms of Eastern Europe. Life in the new country was not much easier, as the settlers were inexperienced farmers and had to contend with malarial swamps, pirate raids and disease.

After five years, the French philanthropist, Baron Edmond de Rothschild, came to the settlers' aid by sending a team of experts to start a vineyard and providing the necessary financial assistance. They arrived armed with shoots of Bordeaux, Beaujolais and Burgundy grapevines and Israel's wine industry was born.

BOTZ, THE BUTCH DRINK

Botz, which means 'mud' in Hebrew, is a very macho kind of coffee drink in Israel. Like Turkish coffee, it's very strong and drunk black. Unlike Turkish coffee, in which the sludge is left at the bottom of the cup, the botz drinker swallows the grounds (the coffee is stirred so the solids float around). If this prospect is too awful, then ask for 'Nes' which is ordinary Nescafé.

The first wines were mainly sweet, made for Jewish religious holidays, but by 1957, when Rothschild relinquished control and the **Carmel Winery** was started. This was the beginning of today's range of delicious dry whites and table wines. Visitors can tour the cellars and enjoy a free tasting. The vineyard's pretty garden contains seven trees from biblical times: fig, date, grape, pomegranate, olive, palm and carob. Centre for Wine Culture at the cellars is open 09:30–17:00 Sun–Thu, 09:00–14:00 Fri.

On the way back to Tel Aviv, visit the beach resort of **Bat Yam** for a swim. The beaches here are broad, clean and surprisingly uncrowded.

Ashkelon ★★

The most southerly resort town along the west coast, Ashkelon has 12km (7 1/2 miles) of beautiful sandy beach. The town is pleasant if modern, but Ashkelon's origins date back 4000 years to when it was an important Philistine city-state. As a trading port on the Via Maris, the coast road linking Egypt and Syria, Ashkelon exported wine and grain. It consequently became much desired by the Assyrians, Babylonians, Greeks, Romans, Arabs and Crusaders. Buildings, statues and columns have been uncovered by archaeologists and there are some awe-inspiring relics casually scattered around (such as the toppled Roman pillars lying in frothy surf at the base of the sand dunes), but as yet the ancient ruins of Ashkelon's original city-state have not been discovered.

National Antiquities Park ★★

Part theme park, part excavations, this shoreside park is littered with ancient pillars, columns and statues. A grassy wall, built by the Crusaders, surrounds the site, while the beach forms the other border. Visitors can wander freely through the ruins and reconstructed **Roman columns** and roads, and look at the **Sculpture Corner** in the park, where some of the archaeologists' finds are displayed.

◀ Left: Succulent olives on sale in Netanya; the town is also well known for citrus fruits.

Painted Tomb ★

Near the town centre, on the beach, is a Roman tomb some 1700 years old, depicting scenes from the afterlife. Although recently restored, it is not yet open to the public due to construction at the nearby marina. Updates via www.ashkelon.muni.il

Herzliya ★★

North of Tel Aviv, the ritzy resort of Herzliya which was named after Theodor Herzl, the founder of Zionism, is the playground of Israel's wealthy. A popular weekend retreat from Tel Aviv for those lucky enough to afford a villa here, Herzliya is packed with gourmet restaurants, deluxe hotels and fashionable cafés, strung out along beautiful beaches crammed with tanning bodies in summer. Some of the beaches charge an entrance fee and some have special functions. **Shefayim** is a nudist beach while, at the other end of the scale, **Separate Beach** is the religious beach. Outside the city, a zone of high-tech companies has sprung up, many of them in the communications business. Plush villas, inhabited by entrepreneurs, line the low hills overlooking the Mediterranean.

People, not ruins, are what visitors come to Herzliya to see, but there is one rather crumbling historical site nearby at **Arshaf**. The Greeks built a port here called **Appollonia**, of which nothing but a part of a jetty remains. There's a 12th-

TEL AVIV

▶ *Right: Israel bears much historical evidence of the times of the Crusaders.*

century Crusader fort nearby, though no signs remain of the battle fought here between Richard the Lionheart and Saladin during the Crusader era. The fort was destroyed later by the Mamelukes. Some people claim the sandy beach contains fragments of purple-coloured glass, dating back to the seventh century AD when a huge factory was built at Hadera, some distance to the north.

Netanya *
Some distance further to the north, Netanya is a bustling and less ostentatious beach resort nestling behind a long line of scrub-covered sand dunes. Netanya is the centre for Israel's two biggest foreign exchange earners, citrus and diamond polishing. The town was founded in 1929 amidst the citrus groves, and the diamond business was brought to Netanya by immigrant Belgian and Dutch Jews, already skilled in polishing and cutting.

In winter, the resort is dead but summer sees a lively cultural programme of international movies, folklore shows and singing in the modern amphitheatre in **Gan Ha-Melekh Park**, right on the beach. As well as water sports, there's horse-riding outside the town. For something different, visitors can see a **citrus-packing plant** in action or have supper with an Israeli family, which can be arranged through the tourist office.

BEST TIMES TO VISIT

Tel Aviv enjoys a **balmy** climate all year round, although summer is best avoided as it can get very **humid** and oppressive. From **April** to **October**, the weather is warm enough to enjoy the beaches and swimming in the Mediterranean. September is the main period of Jewish holidays, during which time many attractions will be closed for the occasional day.

GETTING THERE

Ben Gurion International, Israel's main airport, is situated 20km (12½ miles) from the city, served by buses, trains and taxis. There's a small domestic airport, **Sde Dov**, north of the city, with flights to other parts of Israel. Buses in Tel Aviv are run by **Dan** (tel: 03 639 4444, www.dan.co.il) and **Egged** (tel: 03 694 8888, www.egged.co.il). **Israel Railways** operates frequent trains from the airport to four stops in Tel Aviv, tel: 077 232 4000, www.rail.co.il Taxis wait at the airport and operate on a meter.

GETTING AROUND

Tel Aviv has an efficient **bus** service, run mainly by Dan (see above) and with some Egged buses (www.egged.co.il). **Taxis** are inexpensive and can be hailed on the street. **Walking** is pleasant outside the main summer season; you can walk all the way from north Tel Aviv to Jaffa on the beach. It's not worth hiring a car unless you plan to leave the city and need transport for day trips. **Car Rental:** Avis, 13 Ha-Yarkon St, tel: 03 527 1752; Budget, 99 Ha-Yarkon St, tel: 03 935 0012. Be green and hire a **bicycle** instead, tel: 03 544 2292, www.rentabikeisrael.com

WHERE TO STAY

All the big hotels are along Ha-Yarkon on the beach, for which there is naturally a premium to pay. Tel Aviv also has a good selection of budget accommodation and a youth hostel.

Luxury

InterContinental David Tel Aviv, 12 Kaufman St, tel: 03 795 1111, www.ihg.com City landmark, five-star de luxe hotel on the southern end of the beach promenade, near Old Jaffa.

Dan Tel Aviv, 99 Ha-Yarkon St, tel: 03 520 2525, www.danhotels.com Probably Tel Aviv's most famous hotel, with rooftop pool, contemporary rooms and a legendary breakfast buffet.

Nina Cafe Hotel, 15 Neve Tzedek St, Neve Tzedek, tel: 052 508 4141, www.ninacafehotel.com Gorgeous boutique hotel with just nine beautiful suites attached to one of the trendiest bars, Nina Cafe, in the style of a Parisian coffee house.

Sheraton Hotel, 115 Ha-Yarkon Street, tel: 03 521 1111, www.sheratontelaviv.com Central beachfront location, two restaurants and poolside grill.

Carlton Tel Aviv, 10 Eliezer Peri Street, tel: 03 520 1818, www.carlton.co.il Large five-star business/leisure hotel with a beach restaurant and a swimming pool.

Hilton Tel Aviv, Independence Park, 205 Ha-Yarkon St, tel: 03 520 2222, www.hilton.com/telaviv Long-established five-star business hotel, which also attracts leisure guests thanks to its great location on the beach.

Mid-range

Prima Tel Aviv, 105 Ha-Yarkon St, tel: 03 527 5660, www.prima-hotels-israel.com Moderately priced hotel in enviable beachfront location, with its own kosher Thai restaurant.

Hotel Cinema, 1 Zamenhoff Street, tel: 03 520 7100, www.atlas.co.il Fantastic, characterful hotel at Dizengoff Circle in a former cinema. Old cinema posters and memorabilia are everywhere and the building retains its original Art Deco features.

Hotel Montefiore, 36 Montefiore St, tel: 03 564

6100, www.hotelmonte fiore.co.il Beautiful boutique bolthole in a 1920s mansion with 12 suites and an ultra-trendy bar and restaurant.

Neve Tzedek Hotel, 4 Degania Street, Neve Tzedek, tel: 054 207 0706, www.nevetzedekhotel.com This is a new boutique hotel from the owner of the legendary Nana Bar. It consists of just five suites, each with its own home cinema, Jacuzzi and garden or roof terrace.

Andromeda Hill Hotel, 3 Louis Pasteur St, Jaffa, tel: 03 683 8448, www.andromeda.co.il Luxurious self-catering apartments in a fantastic location in Jaffa. Residents have the use of a pool and a spa.

Budget

Old Jaffa Hostel, 13 Amiad Street, tel: 03 682 2370, www.telaviv-hostel.com Friendly hostel in converted Turkish house, in the middle of the Jaffa flea market. Roof garden overlooking the sea.

Prima City Hotel, 9 Mapu St, tel: 03 524 6253, www.prima-hotels-israel.com Small hotel in a quiet street just off the main promenade.

Maxim Hotel, 86 Ha-Yarkon St, Tel Aviv, tel: 03 517 3721, www.maxim-htl-ta.co.il Recently renovated, this reasonably priced small hotel is situated in the heart of the action, near the nightlife and shopping, right on the beach.

Armon Ha-Yarkon, 268 Ha-Yarkon Street, tel: 03 605 5271, www.armon-hotel.com. This small, 24-room hotel is located within walking distance of the port.

WHERE TO EAT

Tel Aviv has lots of restaurants, offering some of the most creative and exciting cuisine in the Mediterranean. Many are tucked away in Neve Tzedek but there are some superb restaurants along the waterfront and a whole crop of atmospheric places to eat at the New Port. Several of the hotels also offer fine dining. For more casual dining, try Jaffa and the fast-food falafel joints around Carmel Market.

Luxury

Manta Ray, Southern Promenade, tel: 03 517 4773. Stylish and fashionable, right on the beach, serving superb fish dishes and Israeli salads.

Catit, 57 Nahlat Binyamin Street, Neve Tzedek, tel: 03 510 7001. Chic restaurant in beautifully restored old mansion. Power lunches and romantic dinners. Mediterranean specialities.

Sushisamba TLV, 27 Ha-Barzel St, Ramat Ha-Chayal, tel: 03 644 4345. Japanese meets Brazilian and Peruvian cuisine in this ultra-hip outpost of the well-known US restaurant.

Nana Bar, 1 Ahad Ha'am St, Neve Tzedek, tel: 03 516 1915. This ultra-chic bar/ Parisian café is located in trendy Neve Tzedek.

Mid-range

Cordelia Restaurant, 30 Jefet Street, tel: 03 518 4668, www.cordelia.co.il Owned and run by Nir Zook, Israel's celebrity chef so quite pricey. Attached to the Jaffa Bar and the Bistro, forming a corridor between two buildings, with industrial, eclectic design. French and Middle Eastern specialities.

Yaffo Caffè, by Jaffa Flea Market, 11 Olei Zion Street, tel: 03 518 1988, www.yaffocaffe.com Hugely popular café with stark, industrial design and curious flock wallpaper. Very hip. Don't miss the fabulous ice creams – lemon mint, coffee meringue and chocolate orange, for a start.

Orna and Ella, 33 Shenken St, tel: 03 525 2085. A Tel Aviv classic café; very romantic and very fashionable, with French and Mediterranean dishes.

Blackout, Nalaga'at Centre, Jaffa Port, tel: 03 633 0808. Kosher restaurant in Jaffa Port run by blind, deaf and dumb people (the name of the restaurant means 'please touch'), where you can enjoy the unusual experience of dining in the dark.

Buddha Burger, 86 Ibn Gavirol St, tel: 03 522 3040; also at 21 Yehuda Ha-Levi St, tel: 03 510 1222, www.buddhaburgers.co.il Brilliantly creative veggie food is served at this eatery, from salads and burritos to stir fries and 'burgers'.

Budget

Abouelafia, 4 Yefet Street. 24-hour takeaway bakery on the main street, serving absolutely everything — falafel, cakes, slices of pizza, pies, pastries dripping with honey. It's a Jaffa institution. **Dr Shakshuka**, 3 Beit Eshel, Jaffa, tel: 03 682 2842. Local institution, filling a large courtyard by the flea market and packed at lunchtimes on market days. Try the *shak-shuka* — fried egg baked in a spicy tomato sauce, as well as couscous, dips and salads, stews and hearty soups.

SHOPPING

Shenken Street is one of the city's busiest shopping areas, with Israeli designers, boutique interior shops and lots of accessories establishments. For cutting-edge design, wander around the **Gan Ha-Hashmal (Electric Garden)** area (Levontin and Ha-Hashmal streets) where there are lots of up-and-coming clothing and jewellery designers and some amazing leather shops. Bigger and

more mainstream shops are around **Dizengoff Mall**. For fruit, vegetables, souvenirs and general household goods, you can't beat **Carmel Market**. For gifts to take home, art, fun Judaica and pretty household items, **Nahalat Binyamin** market on Friday mornings is best.

TOURS AND EXCURSIONS

Take a city tour in an **open-top bus**, calling at all the main sights, including Old Jaffa (http://city-tour.co.il). There are free walking tours of the **White City** every Saturday, at 11:00. Meet at 46 Rothschild Boulevard (corner of Shadal Street). This tour focuses on the modern architectural styles of the 1930s in one of 'The White City' main areas, along Rothschild Boulevard. There is no need to book in advance. There are also tours from the Tel Aviv Bauhaus Center, 99 Dizengoff St, tel: 03 522 0249, on Fridays at 10:00; www.bauhaus-center.com At 09:30/10:00 on Wednesdays there's a free walking tour of Jaffa in English, starting from the clock tower; tel: 03 603 7700. Big pop and rock

concerts take place in Ha-Yarkon park, many featuring internationally famous bands. Concerts often take place in the open air and the atmosphere at such concerts on a warm night is wonderful.

USEFUL CONTACTS

Ben Gurion International Airport flight information, tel: 03 937 1111.
Tourist Information Offices: Ben Gurion Airport, tel: 03 975 4260; 46 Herbert Samuel St, tel: 03 516 6188; Tel Aviv Jaffa Municipality, Yitzhak Rabin Square, tel: 03 521 8438. Also look out for the new, mobile tourist information booth — blue, green and white Segways, which tour the popular tourist sites dispensing help and information.
Local information:
www.visit-tlv.com
Police, tel: 100.
Magen David Adom First Aid, tel: 101.
Fire Department, tel: 102.
You will find that all the main **car rental** companies have offices in Tel Aviv:
Avis, tel: 03 527 1752;
Budget, tel: 03 935 0012;
Eldan, tel: 03 527 1166/7.

TEL AVIV	J	F	M	A	M	J	J	A	S	O	N	D
AVERAGE TEMP. °F	65	66	68	72	77	83	86	86	89	84	76	66
AVERAGE TEMP. °C	18	19	20	22	25	28	30	30	31	29	24	19
RAINFALL in	3.1	3.1	2.2	.6	0	0	0	0	0	.63	1.9	2.3
RAINFALL mm	80	80	56	15	0	0	0	0	0	16	48	62
Days of rainfall	11	11	8	4	0	0	0	0	0	5	10	11

4
The Dead Sea and Negev

Yet another of Israel's many unusual experiences, the Dead Sea is a must for every visitor. While the water is 'dead' – it harbours no life – the region is immensely beautiful: the yellow mountains of the **Judean Desert** roll into a hazy blue sky, with the occasional splash of brilliant green heralding a kibbutz. Along the shoreline are two deeply important sites: **Qumran**, where the **Dead Sea Scrolls**, the oldest documents known to man, were discovered and tragic **Masada**, the one-time mountain fortress of the ill-fated **Zealots**.

The Judean Desert merges into the dusty **Negev**, which blends into the Egyptian Sinai. The Negev is gaining a reputation for adventure travel such as trekking, camel riding, abseiling and survival excursions. The surprisingly lush wadis (seasonal river beds) are home to all kinds of wildlife, and in places underground springs have been tapped to bring the desert into bloom. In the central Negev, a string of unusual craters, the best known of which is **Makhtesh Ramon** (in the town of Mitzpe Ramon), attracts growing numbers of tourists.

In the far south, where Israel narrows down to the point of a V, is **Eilat**, about as far removed from the country's sombre religious and historical sites as it is possible to get, although sadly it has not proven immune from terrorist attacks. Big, brash and lively, it's packed with tourist hotels and nightlife. Should they so wish, visitors can now fly in and out of the so-called Red Sea Riviera and not go within miles of a temple or ruin for their entire stay.

DON'T MISS

*** Dead Sea: enjoy the Israel cliché: float on the sea.
*** Masada: evocative ruins.
** Eilat: swim with dolphins.
** Desert Safari: see the area by jeep or by camel.
** The Hai-Bar Nature Reserve: great wildlife tours.
** Qumran: the site where the Dead Sea Scrolls were discovered.
** Ein Gedi waterfalls: near the Dead Sea – not to be missed.

◄ *Opposite: The desert becomes harsher and hotter as the road descends to the Dead Sea.*

83

THE DEAD SEA AND NEGEV

THE SALTY SEA

The reason we can **float** on the Dead Sea is because of its concentration of solid substances. Six times as salty as the ocean, the Dead Sea contains 27% of the solids of sodium chloride (common salt), magnesium chloride, calcium chloride, potassium chloride, bromine and more. The lake contains no life except for a few kinds of microbes; sea fish put into its waters soon die. The Dead Sea is economically important as a source of potash, bromine, gypsum, salt, and other chemical products.

▼ *Below: Follow the rules when swimming in the Dead Sea or you may just be in for an unwelcome surprise.*

THE DEAD SEA IS COMPLETELY SAFE IF YOU FOLLOW SOME SIMPLE RULES.

USE THE STEPS WHILE GETTING INTO THE WATER.

FIRST TAKE A SITTING POSITION, AND THEN LIE ON YOUR BACK.

DON'T ATTEMPT ANY BRAEST STROKE. YOUR HEAD MIGHT SINK AND IT'S DANGEROUS.

IF SOME WATER GETS INTO YOUR EYES DON'T PANIC LIE QUIETLY ON YOUR BACK AND THE PAIN WILL PASS.

DON'T SPLASH, ESPECIALLY NOT ON OTHERS.

IT'S STRICTLY FORBIDDEN TO DRINK THE WATER. IF BY MISTAKE YOU SWALLOW SOME WATER GO AT ONCE TO THE OFFICE AND GET A DRINK.

USE ONLY THE MARKED ZONE.

CLOSED ON SABBATH & HOLIDAYS.

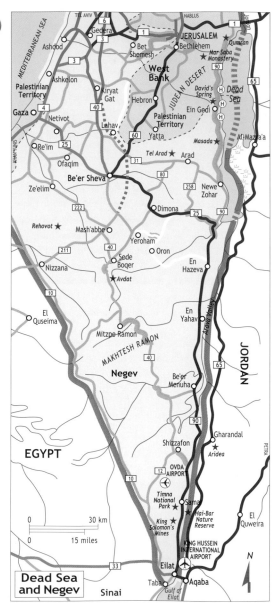

Dead Sea and Negev

THE DEAD SEA

The lowest point on earth at about 400m (1300ft) below sea level, the Dead Sea is fascinating. In winter, the dry air, balmy climate and pure atmosphere make a visit an absolute joy. In summer, as you descend through the mountains from Jerusalem past the sign saying 'sea level', a wall of heat hits you in the face.

The Dead Sea is actually composed of two shimmering blue lakes, linked by a canal, and fed by the **River Jordan** from the north; it is surrounded by steep, barren mountains which turn into an incredible shade of mauve at sunset. Sparkling chunks of salt crystals float on the lake and the shoreline in places consists of glistening black mud, which health-mad tourists delight in slapping all over their bodies. A number of health spas have sprung up along the shores, although the occasional dilapidated ruin sitting in the middle of the bleached desert is testimony to the fact that the lake is shrinking fast, mainly as a result of the construction of Israel's National Carrier system and a similar Jordanian water system, a source of alarm to both Israel and Jordan (which lies along the eastern shore). Israel has created a series of artificial lakes at the south-ern end of the Dead Sea for the extraction of potash, but otherwise the land is used for campsites and health spas, promising to cure everything from arthritis to psoriasis.

In the past the Dead Sea was a short-term visit for all but the most dedicated of spa-goers, but at the southern end a host of modern and luxury hotels with beaches and spas has turned it into a thriving holi-day destination.

EIN GEDI BEACH

No trip to Israel is complete without a swim in the Dead Sea. You float like a cork and it's impossible to keep any body part under water, due to the high salt content. The minerals are supposed to have therapeutic properties but will pickle anyone who stays in too long – it's essential to have a shower after any length of dip. Ein Gedi beach has showers, a spa, several pools, a restaurant and shade.

▼ *Below: Visitors come to relax at the lowest point on earth.*

THE DEAD SEA AND NEGEV

The national park of Ein Gedi has existed since the Bible began; the Song of Songs (1:14), for example, proclaims: 'My beloved to me is a spray of henna blooms from the vineyards of Ein Gedi.' Today, the most important inhabitants are the animals, which range from the **rock hyrax** (like oversized guinea pigs) to foxes, wolves, hyenas, **ibex** and **leopards**. The leopards are highly endangered and rarely seen, emerging at night to prey on partridges, ibex and hyraxes. The ibex are common in comparison. Their mating season lasts from September to October, and in April females can be seen with their young.

Qumran ★★

A network of dusty canyons 100m (300ft) above the Dead Sea, Qumran is where the **Dead Sea Scrolls** were found in 1947. The area was a settlement of the religious sect, the **Essenes**, who wrote the scrolls, and today Qumran has been designated as a national park. A few remains of the settlement can be seen: a tower and a few rooms as well as the pretty oasis of **Ein Feshkha** to the south, where the locals cultivated their vegetable crops. Try to visit at sunset to get a feel for the silence of the desert and the emptiness of the place.

The Essene people who made Qumran their headquarters in around 150BC were a very strict religious sect who lived a simple, monastic lifestyle in all-male communities. Women had to be 'pure' to produce an Essene child and apart from reproduction, had no place in the community. The Essenes predicted the end of the world to be a battle between the Sons of Darkness and the Sons of Light. This idea is illustrated at the Israel Museum in Jerusalem by a black marble slab placed alongside the white Shrine of the Book that today houses the Dead Sea Scrolls.

The scrolls revealed a great deal about Essene life and philosophy and threw new light on the **Second Temple Period**, as well as illustrating anti-Roman feeling among Jews at the time. However, in the first **Jewish War** in AD88, Essene history came to an abrupt end when the sect was tragically wiped out by the Romans. An audiovisual presentation at the visitors' centre tells the whole story (http://old.parks.org.il/). Open 08:00–17:00 Apr–Sep, 08:00–16:00 Oct–Mar.

Ein Gedi ★★

Ein Gedi National Park and Nature Reserve is on the shore of the Dead Sea where the scenery resembles biblical Eden as the icy water of **David's Spring**,

▼ *Below: Heat shimmers off the Dead Sea year-round.*

fringed with green ferns, gushes out of the rock. Not surprisingly, **wildlife** is abundant here and you're bound to see ibex, wild sheep, and hyraxes (small rodent-like animals). Gazelles, oryx, foxes, and jackals also live here but are harder to spot, as are the extremely rare and seldom spotted leopards in the reserve.

David's Spring is busy, particularly so in summer, but there's plenty of hiking amongst the rocks and canyons (remember to take lots of water with you) and in the **Nachal Arugot**, a canyon to the south of the waterfall, there are wonderfully cool rock pools where visitors routinely ignore the signs saying 'no bathing'. The reserve is open 08:00–17:00 Apr–Sep, 08:00–16:00 Oct–Mar.

Ein Gedi is also a good spot for the mandatory dip in the Dead Sea. Only ever swim where there are beach showers, as the crust of minerals left by the evaporating water on your skin acts as an irritant. Attempting to swim can be hilarious. Mobility is virtually impossible and you'll find your feet will keep bobbing up in front of you! Avoid tasting the water – it's foul – and don't get it in your eyes. Anyone with cuts will soon know about it as the salt creates a sharp sting. Also try digging under the sand for the famous black mud, which, when applied all over the body, is supposed to cure aches and pains.

▲ *Above: Refreshing waterfalls turn Ein Gedi into a Garden of Eden.*

DEAD HEALTHY

'Dead' is something of a misnomer; the Dead Sea has all sorts of beneficial properties for health:
• **Skin:** The extra 400m (1300ft) that the sun's rays have to travel means relatively low levels of harmful ultraviolet radiation and many visitors to the area find their acne or psoriasis dries up but their skin doesn't burn.
• **Joints:** Mineral-rich mud helps ease rheumatic or arthritic joints, as does the sensation of weightlessness in the salty water.
• **Asthma:** The evaporating water has a high concentration of oxygen and bromide, easing allergies and asthma.

Masada ★★★

Masada is one of the most spectacular and poignant sites in Israel. A remote table-top mountain with deep *wadis* on each side and the Dead Sea shimmering turquoise in the distance, Masada was the site of the mass suicide by the Zealots in AD73; since then it has been a symbol of national pride.

The earliest fortifications were built here in the 2nd century BC. In AD40, **King Herod** built one of his numerous impenetrable fortresses to serve as a 'bolt hole'. Later, there was a Roman garrison on Masada, but a band of 960 Zealots – men, women and children under the leadership of Elazar

THE DEAD SEA AND NEGEV

▲ *Above: Masada's setting is hauntingly beautiful.*

Ben Yair – stormed Masada in AD66 in an uprising against the Romans and took control of the mountain. Herod had filled the vast water tanks and grain stores for a potential siege and there was plenty for the Zealots to live on, even after the 10,000 Romans – who were camped round the base of the mountain – had cut off the water supply.

After three years of waiting, the Romans started to build a wall around Masada, blocking all possible escape routes, and then constructed a huge, earthern ramp reinforced by wooden beams up to the top of the mountain. They advanced up the ramp with flaming torches and battering rams and the Zealots knew the end was near. Rather than fight the Romans and die as slaves, Elazar Ben Yair decided his people should die with dignity. The men drew lots to decide who would do the deed. Each man killed his family and then himself until just 10 were left. One killed the other nine and then took his own life. Even the Romans, when they broke through the smouldering remains of the walls the next day, admitted admiration for the nobility of the Zealots, as recounted by the historian, Flavius Josephus, in his book, *The Jewish War*.

Nobody can fail to be touched by Masada, which has a gloomy air under the baking sun, even today. You can get to the top by cable car (open 08:00–16:00) or on foot, clambering up the **Snake Path** which has magnificent views, or up the **Battery**, the Romans' ramp (both are open 04:30–17:30; it's important to get to the site early in order to witness the spectacular sunrise!). Sometimes there are long queues for the cable car, but it's worth it just to stand on the top looking down at the Roman encampments and trying to imagine how the Zealots must have felt. The Masada National Park is open Apr–Sep 08:00–17:00, Oct–Mar 08:00–16:00, Fri 1hr earlier.

The excavation of Masada in the 1960s was incredibly exciting, revealing Herod's fortress and later, the more modest accommodation of the Zealots, including their synagogue. In Herod's palace, beautiful mosaics were uncovered revealing patterns of olive branches, vines and pomegranates. There

were also highly sophisticated baths. Climb down into one of the vast water cisterns and marvel at Herod's system of diverting flood water from the wadis to the mountain. Masada continues to stir emotions amongst Israelis today, and a swearing-in ceremony is held here annually for young military recruits who declare: 'Masada shall not fall again'. A sound and light show tells the story of Masada (Mar–Oct, Tue–Thu 21:00); with translations into English (tel: 08 995 9333).

Tel Arad National Park★

West from the Dead Sea, the mountain-top town of Arad is a carefully planned 1960s town. Nearby Tel Arad, an excavated and partly reconstructed Canaanite settlement, is over 5000 years old. A second excavation has revealed a fortress from the 10th century BC, with the remains of a sanctuary modelled on the former Temple in Jerusalem. The Arad Visitors' Centre contains a display of the finds. Open Apr–Sep 08:00–17:00, Oct–Mar 08:00–16:00, Fri 08:00–15:00.

KIBBUTZ LIFE

In the traditional sense, no-one on a kibbutz has any money, and none ever changes hands. Everything is held in a central fund and workers can withdraw cash for 'special' items not supplied by the kibbutz if deemed important. Every night after supper there is a meeting, at which every issue from housekeeping to social issues is debated and decided upon. Children live in a separate house (originally a fortified building where they would be safe from invading Arabs) and spend just a few hours a day with their parents. Women enjoy complete equality. The work, however, is tough. On the agricultural kibbutzim, the working day begins sometimes at 04:00 in summer, with a siesta during the heat of the day. However, with the decline in agriculture and the increase in secondary and tertiary industry that comes with the developed world, the whole existence of the kibbutz in its traditional form is now under threat. Kibbutzim are slowly changing with the times.

▲ Above: Sections of the original tiled floor still remain at Masada.
◄ Left: The ruins of Masada not only bear witness to a remarkable feat of architecture, but also have their own tragic story.

THE DEAD SEA AND NEGEV

▼ *Below: River beds in the Negev Desert make challenging hikes.*

THE NEGEV

Heading west and south from Arad, the Judean Desert becomes the vast Negev, mile upon mile of rocky desert rising into rugged mountains in the south. The Negev occupies 60% of Israel's land but is home to only 10% of its people. The desert does, however, play an important role: defence installations are hidden here; some areas are irrigated and farmed; and there's a handful of ancient sites, dating back thousands of years to when the desert was green and in bloom.

Be'er Sheva *

The capital of the Negev region and Israel's fourth-largest town, Be'er Sheva is a big, busy industrial settlement, mainly Jewish but with a large **Bedouin** population as well. The best feature is the Thursday morning Bedouin Market on the town's southern fringe, a Middle Eastern cacophony of camel trading, goat and sheep auctions, arts and crafts, brass, leather and incense, not to mention its excellent food

stalls selling sticky baklava, dripping with honey. Not surprisingly, the market has become something of a tourist attraction.

Avdat ★★

Due south of Be'er Sheva is the ancient **Nabatean** settlement of Avdat, dating back to the second century BC. The excavations themselves, burial caves, kilns and churches, are interesting but what is really fascinating is the reconstruction of the Nabateans' desert farms. Archaeologists and botanists have rebuilt the Nabateans' unique system of gullies and terraces which collect flash flood water after a storm, and are producing miraculous groves of apricot trees, vines and wheatfields with no additional irrigation.

▲ *Above: A Bedouin woman baking bread in the northern Negev.*

Mitzpe Ramon ★★★

The desert town of Mitzpe Ramon perches on the lip of a vast crater, 40km (25 miles) long and 12km (7½ miles) wide, now designated as a national park. The crater, known as **Makhtesh Ramon**, has expansive vistas across a moon-like landscape of sheer, rocky sides, and its undulating floor of dune-like hills and green wadis. The rock formations are rich in minerals, stained in yellow, purple and red. All sorts of fossilized remains, dating back 200 million years, have been found here.

Today, Mitzpe Ramon is an activity centre, with people **hang-gliding** off the top of the crater walls, **abseiling** down the sides and **horse-trekking** across the floor. You can also hire **camels** for a short trek along the crater rim. Despite the snorting and spitting of the camels, this is a wonderfully peaceful way to soak up the dramatic scenery. If you're travelling with children, visit the nearby **Alpaca Farm**, where llamas and alpaca can be petted (www.alpaca.co.il).

FIRST PM OF ISRAEL

David Ben-Gurion (1886–1973) dedicated his life to establishing a Jewish homeland in Palestine. He left his native Poland in 1906 to work on a farm in a Jewish settlement in Turkish Palestine. In 1910 he became editor of the Zionist workers' newspaper, *Achdut*. In 1930 he formed the Mapai, the Zionist labour party. Throughout World War II, Ben-Gurion battled to allow Jews to immigrate to Palestine, and he became the first prime minister of the new Israel. He remained in the Knesset until his retirement from politics in 1970. For the last 10 years of his life he lived at Sede Boqer, a kibbutz in the Negev. He died here in 1973.

THE DEAD SEA AND NEGEV

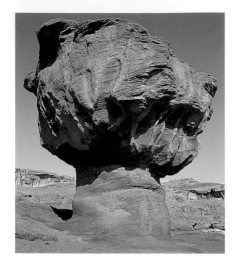

▲ *Above: The bizarre Mushroom in Timna National Park.*

Hai-Bar Nature Reserve ★★

Particularly beautiful is the **Arava Valley**, with the Negev to the west and the Edom Mountains of Jordan to the east. The mountains here are a brilliant shade of pinky-red, changing to orange and purple at sunset. Rocks have been wind-blasted into peculiar shapes and desert creatures shelter from the sun in the gullies and *wadis*.

The Hai-Bar Biblical Wildlife Reserve at **Kibbutz Samar** in Yotvata is one of the game parks in Israel where species from the time of the Bible have been reintroduced. A captive breeding programme aims eventually to release the animals into the wild. With eyes peeled, it's possible to spot wolves, hyenas, ibex, cheetahs and leopards, many of which roamed free until relatively recently; a number were killed by Bedouin who saw them as a threat to their herds. You can drive around the reserve in a car and see the other 450 resident species in the enclosed area. Open Sun–Thu 08:30–17:00, Fri–Sat 08:30–16:00.

Timna National Park ★★

About 30km (20 miles) north of Eilat is Timna National Park, which includes the 6000-year-old King Solomon's mines, once worked by the ancient Egyptians, and later by King Solomon's slaves. Copper ore was roasted in vast ovens after being dug from underground galleries. There are also some weird rock formations, notably **Solomon's Pillars**, a series of huge, rose-pink rock columns, and the **Mushroom**, a massive boulder resting on a sandstone pillar. A full-sized model of the Tabernacle was added in 1999 complete with Ark, Golden Lampstand and Altar of Incense, while a multimedia presentation explains the exodus. You can visit the remains of the Egyptian sanctuaries where the mine workers lived, and see ancient rock carvings.

EILAT

Israel's southernmost point is crammed into a tiny strip of Red Sea beach, dedicated to sun, sea, sand and scuba. To the west is the Egyptian border post of Taba and the sandy expanse of the Sinai; to the east, the Jordanian port of Aqaba and, beyond, the rugged mountains of Saudi Arabia falling into the deep blue sea. The 'riviera' lights up at night, with distant pinpricks from four different countries reflected in the water.

Under its fun-loving veneer, **Eilat** is vital to Israel, providing access to the Red Sea. Many of the young Israelis in town are part of the Israeli Defense Force.

Eilat's past is not particularly illustrious. Moses passed through and King Solomon built a port called Etziongeber. The Queen of Sheba quite probably landed here, followed by various invaders, among them Syrians and Edomites, wresting Eilat from one another over the years. By the time **Lawrence of Arabia** passed through en route to Jordan during World War I (1914–18), Eilat was little more than a collection of fishing shacks.

When Israel became an official nation in 1948, troops were sent quickly to defend the new country's only link to Asia, Africa and Iran – important as sources of oil. Prior to the 1967 Six Day War, Eilat was under tremendous threat from Egypt and Jordan, but Israel's pre-emptive strike and subsequent seizing of the Sinai sent the Egyptians packing. Continued Jordanian terrorist attacks prevented any kind of tourism from developing, until veiled threats from Israel forced them to tighten up border security. Thereafter, Eilat began to boom, with hotels springing up along its North Beach, divers flocking to its lovely underwater reefs, and sun-lovers from chilly northern Europe pouring out of charter aircraft at the nearby Ovda Airport in search of winter warmth.

NOMADS OF THE DESERT

Bedouin are nomadic Arabic tribes, scattered across the mountains and deserts of the Middle East, and in Israel they inhabit the **Negev Desert**. Their homes are goatskin tents, and their lives are spent herding goats, camels and sheep. Bedouin are incredibly hospitable and should you come across a tribe, invitations will be extended to share their lamb and rice, not to mention other parts of the sheep. More and more Bedouin are being settled in houses (and own cars) however, and the traditional way of life is disappearing.

▼ *Below: Sun-drenched Eilat has become a top holiday destination for Israelis.*

▲ *Above: Eilat shares in the underwater treasures of the Red Sea.*
▶ *Opposite: The Underwater Observatory Marine Park at Coral Beach provides visitors with a glimpse of a living reef without getting wet.*
▼ *Below: Eilat's slender strip of beach is what many visitors come for.*

North Beach ★★

The focal point of Eilat is North Beach, a sandy strip backed by a palm-lined promenade and a string of deluxe hotels. The town spreads back over the hills from here, although visitors need stray no further to find restaurants, nightlife and duty-free shopping. Because space on the crowded beach is limited, a lagoon has been built behind the front line of hotels so that others, too, can claim a waterfront position.

Unlike neighbouring Coral Beach, where water sports are banned to protect the shallow reefs, North Beach is not a designated national park and visitors can **swim**, **sail** and **windsurf** from the sand. Regular **boat trips** operate from the **marina** and a sunset cruise is well worth the effort to watch the incredible changing colours of the desert from the water.

Underwater Observatory Marine Park ★★★

Down towards the Egyptian border is Coral Beach, 6km (4 miles) out of town. A couple of luxury hotels are located here, but because the coral reefs are just a metre or so offshore,

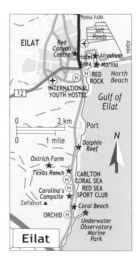

water sports are not an option. The **Underwater Observatory**, however, is outstanding and well worth a visit. The observatory is built under the water; descend the spiral staircase inside the white tower and admire the incredible marine life: corals in rainbow colours with orange, yellow, scarlet and electric-blue fish flitting by, and purple fronds waving in the gentle current. Elsewhere there are sharks and rays contained in an enclosure.

Visitors who want to try snorkelling can visit the **Coral Reserve** nearby, where underwater markers take you on a trail across the reef. The Observatory is open daily 08:30–16:00.

Coral 2000 ★★

Part of the Underwater Observatory at Coral Beach is the very advanced *Coral 2000* boat, with 48 large windows in its hull 1.5m (5ft) below the water level. Sightseeing cruises last 35 minutes and depart at 11:00 and 13:00 Mon–Sat (reservations tel 08 636 4200).

PARTING OF THE SEAS

The Red Sea occupies a portion of the East African Rift Valley, a geological fault along which the earth's crust has been ripping apart for more than 50 million years. The Red Sea formed when the Arabian peninsula was torn from Africa 20 million years ago. It is 2253km (1400 miles) long, up to 2134m (7000ft) deep and just 354km (220 miles) wide at its broadest point, although geologists have found evidence on the sea floor that proves that the Red Sea is still, very slowly, getting wider. The site where the waters miraculously parted to allow the Israelites and Moses to cross is believed to be the Gulf of Suez.

THE DEAD SEA AND NEGEV

Dolphin Reef ★★★

Located on South Beach, between Coral World and the hotel area of North Beach, Dolphin Reef is an area where semi-wild dolphins turn up daily to be fed. Visitors can stand on a platform to watch the dolphins appearing through an opening in the underwater nets that enclose the area. They leap out of the water and perform tricks, even though the staff insist the dolphins have not been trained. There's also no guarantee that they will come every day. For an extra fee, visitors can go snorkelling alongside the dolphins and for yet another fee (you need to book in advance, www.dolphinreef.co.il), you may dive with them. Failing this, there's a pleasant café with outdoor seating and a small sandy beach for sunbathing. Open daily 09:00–17:00, but check first, tel: 08 630 0100/1.

Kings City ★

An attraction in the Eastern Lagoon for all the family, Kings City is a biblically themed amusement park set inside a palace. There are mazes, slides, a 4D film and caves with animated models depicting important scenes from the Bible. The main attraction is the King Solomon's Falls, a dramatic boat ride that takes you through animatronic scenes of the biblical king's life and ends with a splash in the lake outside. Open Sun–Thu 10:00–19:00, Fri 10:00–18:00, but check first, tel: 08 630 4444.

▼ *Below: For those tempted to take up scuba diving, Eilat is a good learning ground, with plenty of training facilities on offer.*

Bird-watching ★★★

Eilat is a bird-watcher's dream since it is situated on the main migration route from Europe to North Africa. In spring and autumn, tales of sightings reach almost biblical proportions as thousands of pelicans, eagles, kites and buzzards darken the skies over Eilat.

The **Israel Nature Protection Authority**, which has an office in the King Solomon Hotel, has set up special trails for bird-watchers and has also installed hidden observation points for watching the lagoon birds. There are slide shows, lectures and nature films on offer too during the migration season.

Desert Adventures ★★★

Various companies run safaris into the Negev from Eilat These include four-wheel-drive excursions along the *wadis*, **quad-biking** along

off-road trails, **horse-riding**, **camel trekking** and **climbing** opportunities. One of the best hikes is the **Red Canyon**, accessible with a guide, where you scramble down a gorge, its rocks smoothed by water over millions of years. For part of the walk you hang on to ropes and metal footholds, while at points you can actually slide down the shiny rock on your backside!

▲ *Above: Petra's ancient amphitheatre, carved into the rock.*
▼ *Below: The sheer scale of the structures at Petra is breathtaking.*

EXCURSIONS BEYOND ISRAEL
Egyptian Sinai ★

Tour companies in Eilat arrange side-trips into the Egyptian Sinai to visit **St Catherine's Monastery**, **Mount Sinai** – where **Moses** received the **Ten Commandments** while leading the Israelites through the desert – and, for divers, the Egyptian coastal resort of **Sharm el-Sheikh**. Visitors can also cross the border (without the need for a visa) at Taba to use the beach and facilities of the Hilton.

Petra ★★★

Jordan's breathtaking 'rose-red city' is fast becoming a popular side-trip now that the Arava border post at Aqaba – a few minutes' drive from Eilat – is open. The trip is quite arduous; but the ancient capital of the Nabateans is so astonishing, carved as it is into a sheer, rose-coloured rock face at the end of a deep rock fissure, that the trip is worthwhile. Several hotels have opened recently to cater for the increasing number of tourists.

THE DEAD SEA AND NEGEV AT A GLANCE

Best Times to Visit

Eilat is a **year-round** resort with very hot, dry summers and mild winters. In summer, the resort is popular with Israelis and in winter, numerous holiday-makers arrive from northern Europe. Winter evenings are chilly, so be sure to bring warm clothes. The **Dead Sea**, meanwhile, is perfect in **winter**, when you can experience mild, dry weather. **Spring** and **autumn** are also good times to visit. Avoid the middle of summer, though, which is punishingly hot and humid.

Getting There

The **Dead Sea** lies between the **international airports** of Tel Aviv and Eilat. From Tel Aviv, the **drive** takes about 90 minutes, or alternatively you can drive from Jerusalem which takes half an hour. **Eilat** is about three hours' drive further south, or a 60-minute flight from Tel Aviv on **Israir**, www.israirairlines.com Eilat itself has an international airport at Ovda, tel: 1700 705 022, which is 40 minutes' drive away, and a domestic airport, tel: 1700 705 022, in the middle of the town. Charter flights from all over Europe serve Ovda, and El Al operates direct flights. **Egged buses** run scheduled services between Jerusalem, Tel Aviv and Eilat and there are **car rental** companies in Eilat. *See* Useful Contacts for phone numbers.

Getting Around

Getting around the **Dead Sea** is possible by public bus, **hire car** or **tour bus**. Taxis, **buses** (**Egged**, tel: 03 694 8888, www.egged.co.il) and *sherut* serve the urban areas of **Eilat** and several companies in the area run 4WD excursions into the desert. Visitors should not drive off-road in the desert. Camel caravan tours allow you to see the desert at a slower pace! Regular excursions run to **Petra** in Jordan, with an Israeli vehicle taking you to the border and a Jordanian vehicle picking you up on the Jordanian side.

Where to Stay
DEAD SEA
Luxury
Isrotel Dead Sea Hotel & Spa, Ein Bokek, tel: 08 668 9666, www.isrotel.com Spectacular modern hotel with excellent leisure facilities and the country's best spa.
Herod's Hotel Dead Sea, Ein Bokek, tel: 08 659 4221, www.leonardohotels.com Luxury hotel on the beach with spa centre.
Leonardo Club Hotel, Dead Sea, tel: 08 668 9444, www.leonardo-hotels.com 388-room hotel with private beach and spa centre.

Mid-range
Ein Gedi Country Hotel, Ein Gedi, tel: 07 659 4221, eg@ein-gedi.org.il Kibbutz with a swimming pool and sports facilities as well as a shuttle service to the Ein Gedi Spa.

Budget
Youth Hostel, on the shores of the Dead Sea, tel: 02 594 5600, www.iyha.org.il Facilities include rooms with air conditioning, coffee and TV; some with views.
Masada Youth Hostel, at the foot of Masada, tel: 02 594 5600, www.iyha.org.il Facilities include rooms with air conditioning, pool, café and a picnic area.

EILAT

Eilat hotels are big, brash and modern, so don't expect anything rustic. Most are situated in the North Beach area where the beachfront is at a premium, while lower-grade establishments are set back from the sea.

Luxury
Herod's Boutique Hotel, North Beach, tel: 08 638 0000, www.leonardohotels.com On private beach, great sea views. Near marina and important Eilat sites.
Isrotel Royal Beach, North Beach, tel: 08 636 8888, www.isrotelexclusivecollection.com/royal_beach Large resort hotel, modern luxuries, on the North Beach.
Dan Eilat, North Beach, Eilat, tel: 08 636 2222, daneilat@danhotels.com Modern Dan property next to the Royal Beach. Five-star luxury.

Mid-range
Orchid, South Beach, Eilat, tel: 08 636 0360, www.orchidhotel.co.il/en/ This is an unusual Thai-style development, near the Underwater Observatory. It offers comfortable bungalow accommodation.
Isrotel Yam Suf Hotel, Coral Beach, tel: 08 638 2222, www.isrotel.com Recently renovated, built around a pool complex, offers diving facilities.

Budget
International Youth Hostel, Arava Road, Eilat, tel: 02 594 5611, www.iyha.org.il Located in town, one block back from the beach. Facilities include a shop, TV room, rooms with air conditioning and a café.

WHERE TO EAT
You will find that there is very little tourist infrastructure along the Dead Sea; therefore most restaurants are located in hotels and *kibbutzim*.
Day-trippers can eat lunch at any of the hotels – the Leonardo Plaza, for example, has five restaurants alone. In Eilat everything from pizza to pancakes, French to Thai cuisine, is available, often with live entertainment.

EILAT
The Last Refuge, Almog Beach, tel: 08 637 3627.

Reputation for seafood.
Red Sea Star, tel: 08 634 7777. Fantastic aquatic theme restaurant 5m (16ft) below the water level with views of the fish swimming past.
Dolphin Reef Café, tel: 08 637 1846. Laid-back beach café at Dolphin Reef with evening entertainment.

SHOPPING
Eilat is a duty-free zone and has great shopping buys such as perfume, jewellery and electronic goods. Shopping in the Dead Sea area is limited, though the Dead Sea beauty products are of excellent quality, available from the spas. The best market in the region is the Bedouin Market in Be'er Sheva on Thursday.

TOURS AND EXCURSIONS
Tour companies based in Eilat include **Egged**, tel: 03 694 8888; **Desert Eco Tours**, tel: 522 765 753, www.desertecotours.com Trips operate to the Dead Sea and Masada, and to Jerusalem. Various 4WD tours operate into the desert, usually including hiking and camel riding. All the tour operators sell trips to Petra in Jordan, using

Jordanian buses and guides from the Jordanian side of the Arava border crossing, outside Eilat.
Scuba diving: Aqua Sport (Coral Beach, tel: 08 633 4404). Snuba (tel: 08 637 2722) offers guided snorkelling tours. Dolphin Reef, tel: 08 630 0111 (telephone the Dolphin Reef several weeks in advance to book a dive with dulphins).
Masada Sound and Light Show, tel: 08 995 9333, arrive 30min before show.

USEFUL CONTACTS
Dead Sea Tourist Information Office, www.deadsea.co.il.
Qumran Visitors Centre, tel: 02 994 2235.
Arad Tourist Information Office, tel: 08 995 4160.
Eilat Tourist Centre, tel: 08 630 9111.
Eilat SPNI Field School (bird-watching), tel: 08 637 2021.
Car rental companies in Eilat include:
Thrifty, tel: 08 699 8877; Budget, tel: 03 694 8888; Hertz, tel: 08 637 5050.
National Parks Protection Authority, http://old.parks.org.il

EILAT	J	F	M	A	M	J	J	A	S	O	N	D
AVERAGE TEMP. °F	59	63	68	77	79	88	90	91	88	79	72	63
AVERAGE TEMP. °C	15	17	20	25	26	31	32	33	31	26	22	17
RAINFALL in	0	0	0	0	0	0	0	0	0	0	0	0
RAINFALL mm	5	5	4	3	1	0	0	0	0	3	4	6
Days of rainfall	1	1	1	0	0	0	0	0	0	0	0	1

5
Galilee

A far cry from the stony Negev or the stark mountains around the Dead Sea, Galilee is composed of green, rolling hills, with the snowy cap of **Mount Hermon** in the distance, the whole juxtaposed against the shimmering blue of the **Sea of Galilee**. Israel's beautiful north is a place to refresh mind, body and soul.

Just 157km (97 miles) from Jerusalem, Galilee is a popular summer holiday centre for Israelis, despite the humidity. The area is also of deep importance to Christians, who flock to the sites where Jesus is said to have performed eight miracles, to see his home town of **Nazareth**, to visit the holy **Mount Tabor**, and to be baptized in the **River Jordan**.

Jews, meanwhile, visit **Safed**, a beautiful old town in the hills — much of it unchanged since the 16th century — and site of the tombs of many important Jewish scholars. Bird-watchers descend on the **Hula Valley** to study the spectacular annual migration, whilst adventurers take to the skies in hang-gliders, to the saddle for leisurely trekking or to the foaming waters of the river in inflatable rafts.

Galilee's main holiday centre is the lakeside town of **Tiberias**, famous for its curative **hot springs**. In addition to hotels and holiday villages, there are several excellent **kibbutzim** around the lake which accept visitors. In winter there's a **ski resort** on Mount Hermon, part of the range that forms the brooding mass of the **Golan Heights**, the battle-scarred buffer zone between Israel and neighbouring Syria.

Don't Miss

*** Beit She'an: explore the Roman excavations.
*** Ancient biblical sites: drive round the lake and visit fascinating biblical sites.
** Jordan River Park: river rafting and kayaking are on offer for the adventurous.
** Capernaum: discover the place where Jesus did much of his preaching.
* Banias: hike in the Golan Heights.
* Vered Hagalil Ranch: enjoy the pleasures of horse-riding here.

◄ *Opposite: Tiberias is now a thriving resort on the Sea of Galilee.*

GALILEE

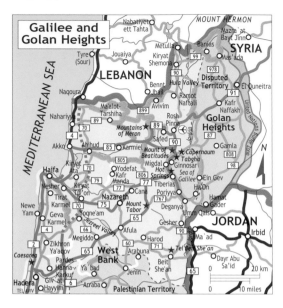

Galilee and Golan Heights

TIBERIAS

On the surface, Tiberias is a fun-loving resort, spread out along the banks of the lake, its promenade lined with outdoor fish restaurants and its marina packed with pleasure cruisers. This is, however, one of Israel's four Jewish holy cities, along with **Safed**, **Jerusalem** and **Hebron**, and several important Jewish scholars are buried here, among them the 12th-century philosopher Moses Maimonides.

Tiberias was founded by Herod the Great's son, Herod Antipas, in AD20 and by the seventh century had become a thriving academic centre. Battling Muslims and Crusaders largely destroyed it in the 12th century and a massive earthquake in 1837 finished off the remainder of the ancient buildings. Consequently, Tiberias is now very much a modern resort with a few crumbling remains scattered around.

SEA OF KINNERET

The Sea of Galilee was once part of a great inland sea extending from the Hula marshes in northern Israel to a point some 64km (40 miles) south of the Dead Sea. The lake is encircled by sandy beaches and bordered by escarpments on the east and southwest and by plains on the north and northwest. The water is cool and clear and contains many species of fish, notably sardines and tilapia, which are sold in the many fish restaurants around the lake. The grebe, gull, pelican, and other species of birds are abundant while animal life includes tortoise, turtle, crayfish and a small crustacean known as the beach flea.

Things to see include the old city walls, best preserved near the Leonardo Plaza Hotel, and a former Turkish citadel in the northwest corner of town, near the historic Dona Gracia Hotel. Tombs include those of **Moses Maimonides** and of the great Jewish thinker **Rabbi Akiva**, who was executed by the Romans in AD 135.

Sadly since 2014 the dazzling fountains leaping to classical music and lasers, against screens featuring historical tableaus, dance no longer. Often compared to the show at the Bellagio Hotel, Las Vegas, the themes were controversial to local religious groups. It's also worth getting up at dawn, when the lake is usually like a sheet of glass, and watching the fishing boats bringing back their haul, just as they did in ancient biblical times.

Tiberias Hot Springs ★★

Built on the lake shore, this spa complex covers a fault that has caused 17 hot, sulphuric springs to gush up from 2000m (6561ft) below the earth's crust at temperatures of up to 60°C (140°F). There are thermal pools, mud wraps, massage, hydrotherapy and Jacuzzi baths for visitors to enjoy, despite the rather pungent smell in the air of sulphuric gases.

The ruins of ancient Jewish city, **Hammath Tiberias** were discovered next to the springs and include exquisite mosaics among the remains of a 4th-century synagogue. (National park, tel: 04 672 5287).

MAN OF LETTERS

Moses Maimonides was born in Spain in 1135 and was a leading sage of his time. He studied medicine in Cairo and became a leading court physician. His greatest achievement was the writing of the *Mishnah Torah*, a document which simplified the whole of Jewish teaching and belief from the *Talmud*. He also wrote the *Guide of the Perplexed*, a presentation of the philosophy of Judaism. He was buried in Tiberias in 1204 and his tomb on Rabbi Abulafiya Street is an important pilgrimage site.

GALILEE

MIRACLES OF GALILEE

Many significant episodes from the **New Testament** happened in the Galilee region. They include:
• The Annunciation – when the Angel told Mary of Nazareth that she would bear the Son of God.
• The miracle of turning water into wine.
• The feeding of the 5000.
• The miracle of walking on the water.
• The miracle of the Gaderene Swine.
• The Transfiguration – when the prophets Moses and Elijah appeared to Jesus and his disciples on Mount Tabor.

AROUND THE LAKE

The Sea of Galilee is surprisingly small – just 50km (36 miles) in circumference. A good road runs right round the lake, hugging the shore and passing through various points of interest. Even if you don't stop much, the scenery is stunning and the countryside unspoilt. In summer the weather is very humid (the lake is actually 120m, or 390ft, below sea level) and there are plenty of swimming places. Spend the day at a leisurely pace and remember to try the delicious St Peter's fish, a freshwater species from the lake named, of course, after St Peter, one of the apostles.

There are several ways to get around the lake: by **car**; by **bicycle**, which can be hired in Tiberias; by **foot**, stopping for the night in one of the kibbutzim along the way; or by **bus**. **Ferries** also travel across the lake to **Ein Gev** on the east coast, a route serious swimmers attempt once a year in a challenge race.

Heading north from Tiberias, the road looks down on the dazzling white rooftops of **Migdal**, birthplace of Mary Magdalene. Just beyond here is the **Kibbutz Ginosar**, which harbours an amazing find: an old fishing boat, discovered in the mud at the bottom of the lake when the water was low. The boat has been dated as 2000 years old, so would probably have been in use during the time of Jesus.

A little further on at **Tabgha** is a Byzantine-style basilica, the **Church of the Multiplication**, built in 1981 (incorporating its 5th-century predecessor) with beautiful mosaic floors depicting flora and birds. At the front of the altar is a mosaic of the loaves and fishes, alluding to the biblical story of the feeding of the 5000. Open 08:00–17:00 Mon–Fri, 08:00–15:00 Sat, 09:00 (briefly) Sun.

▼ Below: The synagogue in Capernaum is 1700 years old.

From here, follow the signs to the **Mount of Beatitudes**, where an Italian church (constructed in 1937) marks the spot of the Sermon on the Mount. Open 08:00–11:30, 14:30–16:30 daily.

At the northern end of the lake, **Capernaum** is the ancient town where Jesus did much of his preaching. Several of his disciples, including Peter, are believed to have come from here. In AD 700 the town was destroyed after the Arab conquest. Two excavated sites are worth visiting: **St Peter's House**, (incorporated within an old and a new church) and next to it, a 1700-year-old synagogue. National park open 08:00–17:00 Sun–Thu, church: tel: 04 672 0516.

▲ *Above: Pilgrims come from around the world to be baptized in the River Jordan.*

The eastern side of the lake is much less developed, with a string of sandy beaches and a few holiday villages. You can stop and swim or rent a boat at the **Kibbutz Ein Gev**, about halfway down. A short detour towards the Jordanian border leads to **Hamat Gader**, another hot spring, which has remained popular since Roman times. The spring has been channelled into a pool and there's plenty of black mud which is reputed to be very beneficial for your skin. Also of interest here are some impressive Roman ruins and an amphitheatre, and if you're trailing fractious children around the historic sites, there is the unexpected treat of an alligator farm! As an added bonus, the **Kibbutz Ha'On** on the lake shore has an ostrich farm.

On the southwestern shore, at the point where the River Jordan leaves the lake, is the spot where John the Baptist is believed to have baptized Jesus so that he could set out on his mission. Now there's a specially constructed baptismal site here where white-robed pilgrims line up to be submerged in the water in order to be spiritually 'cleansed'.

SAINT MARY

Mary Magdalene was born in Migdal on the shores of the Sea of Galilee. She is thought to have been a prostitute and is referred to in the Bible as a 'sinning woman'. Jesus healed her of evil spirits and she became a devout follower, anointing his feet and keeping a vigil at the foot of the cross during the crucifixion. It was to Mary Magdalene that Jesus appeared after his resurrection. She is remembered as a saint and her feast day on the Christian calendar is July 22.

GALILEE

▲ *Above: Nazareth, once a tiny village, is a sprawling town nowadays.*

NAZARETH

Once a tiny, rustic village, Nazareth comes as something of a surprise. It is now a slightly unattractive, sprawling town, with a large Christian Arab population living mainly in the old area, and a modern section, **Natzeret Illit**, populated by Jews. Nazareth was the home of the Holy Family, and churches, basilicas and convents have sprung up everywhere to commemorate even the most minor happenings. The town is an essential pilgrimage for Christians and is always busy with tour buses.

Basilica of the Annunciation ★★

A modern, imposing church built in 1966, this basilica covers the spot where Mary's house would have stood, and on which Byzantine and Crusader churches were built. Its unusual dome dominates the skyline of Nazareth. Inside, brightly coloured murals from different countries depict the Annunciation. Stroll from here down Pilgrim's Walk, created for the Millennium celebrations, to Mary's Well, site of Mary's first encounter with the Archangel Gabriel. Open 08:00–18:00 daily (summer). Mass held Sunday.

St Joseph's Church ★

Across the square is the more modest St Joseph's Church, built over a cavern which is believed to have been Joseph's carpentry workshop. Open 07:00–18:00.

St Gabriel Greek Orthodox Church ★★

Up the hill heading out of town is the spot where Greek Orthodox belief has it that the Angel Gabriel appeared to Mary while she was fetching water. The 17th-century church – with ancient stones remaining from three earlier churches – is built over an underground spring connected by a subterranean aqueduct to Mary's Well, believed to contain water with curative properties. Open 08:00–12:00, 13:00–17:00 Mon–Sat.

Cana ∗

A few miles north of Nazareth is Cana, where Jesus is supposed to have performed his first miracle – that of turning water into wine. The village today, surrounded by pomegranate groves, is populated by Arabs; it has two churches, a Franciscan and a Greek Orthodox Church, both marking the supposed site of the miracle. Cana is easily accessible from Nazareth and a bus runs every 45 minutes.

THE JEZREEL VALLEY

With a car, it's possible to make a leisurely meander around the lush and rather dramatic-looking Jezreel Valley. The road climbs up **Mount Tabor** and winds down again to dramatic Roman remains in **Beit She'an**, from where you can head back up the Jordan River Valley to Tiberias.

Mount Tabor ∗∗

Mount Tabor, 18km (11 miles) southwest of **Tiberias**, has been an important religious site since the Canaanites first inhabited this area. Sacrifices were performed here and an ancient shrine to the pagan god, Baal, can still be seen in the rock face below the **Church of the Transfiguration**, high up on the mountain. The Canaanites were defeated by the prophet Deborah, according to the Book of Judges, who led an army of 10,000 Israelites to victory on this mountain.

According to a 4th-century interpretation of the Book of Luke, Mount Tabor is where the **Transfiguration** took place. Here Jesus appeared to the apostles, transfigured, his garments a dazzling white, as he spoke to the prophets Moses and Elijah.

If it's not too hot, walk up the 3km (2-mile) dirt road to the beautiful **Church of the Transfiguration** built in 1924 (buses are no longer allowed to drive up here). Open 08:00–12:00, 14:00 to sunset Sun–Fri. The views down over the valley are impressive and inside the church is a gold mosaic of the Transfiguration. Nearby, there's a ruined Arab castle, dating back to the 13th century.

GAN HASHLOSHA NATIONAL PARK

In the Beit She'an Valley is Gan Hashlosha (or Sachne, Arabic for 'warm'), a beautifully landscaped area with a natural swimming pool fed by springs as its central feature. The springs keep the water at 28ºC (82ºF) so it's great for a swim even in winter. The pool is divided by gentle waterfalls, ideal for splashing around in and safe for children. A snack bar and changing room are on site. Open 08:00–17:00 (Apr–Sep), 08:00–16:00 (Oct–Mar).

▲ *Above: Visitors can wander among the excavations at Tel Beit She'an; an earthquake in AD749 is thought to have led to the collapse of columns on the main avenue.*

Tel Beit She'an ★★

Following the Jezreel Valley to the east you reach the spectacular Roman remains of Tel Beit She'an, rivalling Caesarea in magnitude. A huge **Roman amphitheatre** has been excavated, as well as a gymnasium, a theatre seating 7000, a temple and a broad avenue, or cardo, lined with columns believed to have toppled in an earthquake in AD749. A multisensory sound and light show, She'an Nights, tells the story and includes such special effects as meeting historical characters and feeling the earthquake. Open 08:00–17:00 (until 16:00 in winter) Sun–Thu and Sat; 08:00–16:00 (until 15:00 in winter) Fri. Book in advance for the She'an Nights show, tel: 1 222 3639.

SAFED

Charming and atmospheric, the ancient hill town of Safed nestles in front of the **Mountains of Meron**. One of the four Jewish holy cities, Safed has great religious significance and attracts many visitors. Although Safed doesn't appear in the Bible, it contains the tomb of Rabbi Shimon Bar-Yochai who in the second century wrote the *Cabala* (or *Kabbalah*), an ancient text of Judaism. The *Schulchan Aruch*, a set of rules by which Jews live their daily lives, was later written here.

Safed enhanced its position as a seat of learning in the 16th century as thousands of intellectual Spanish Jews fleeing the Inquisition settled here. Schools and synagogues prospered until an earthquake in 1759 destroyed most of the buildings. The town only came back to life with the arrival of a large group of **Hassidic Jews** from Eastern Europe, the descendants of whom live here today in the belief that the Messiah will descend from the Mountains of Meron to Safed before making an appearance in Jerusalem.

The unspoilt scenery and clear air have attracted many artists, who inhabit a maze of narrow lanes in the Old Town, known as the **Artists' Quarter**. Here visitors can browse through creative art displays that start with micro-calligraphy, photography and painting, progressing through sculpture, ceramics and jewellery design. Safed also has a large

THE LEGENDS OF SAFED

The ancient town of Safed is steeped in legend. One tale is of a 16th-century poet, returning to his home after a long journey. A group of bandits accosted him and threatened to kill him, finally allowing him one last request. The poet started to play a beautiful melody on his flute which sent the bandits' camels into a trance. The camels started to dance and the terrified bandits fled.

number of synagogues, some of which survived the town's many earthquakes. The oldest, Bana's Synagogue, dates back to the 15th century.

THE GOLAN HEIGHTS

A massive slab of uplifted basalt, the Golan Heights form the strategically vital northeast corner of Israel, Lebanon and Syria and remain a huge stumbling block in the Israel–Syria peace talks. The national parks are safe for visitors but some of the remote mountainous areas still contain land mines: hike only with a guide.

Gamla *

A few kilometres northeast of the **Sea of Galilee**, the town of Gamla experienced a tragic repetition of Masada, during the same revolt against the Romans in AD66. Over 9000 Zealots died. Some 4000 were killed by advancing Roman troops and after a long siege, the remaining 5000 committed suicide by jumping off the jagged cliffs to their death. The Romans destroyed the town but archaeologists discovered its remains in 1968 and visitors can wander around the eerie excavations, while a colony of massive griffon vultures wheels overhead.

Banias **

The springs and waterfalls at Banias in the far north, one of the main sources of the River Jordan, have been worshipped since long before biblical times, when gods were believed to dwell in trees, rivers and rocks. Primitive shrines hollowed out of the rock once probably contained effigies of the Greek god Pan (Panaeas) from whose name Banias derives. Muslims later associated the place with Elijah. Today, as Hermon Stream Nature Reserve, there are well-marked hiking trails. Open 08:00–16:00 (winter), 08:00–17:00 (summer), closes 1hr earlier Fri.

> **SKIING ON MOUNT HERMON**
>
> Mount Hermon is somehow an unlikely place to find a **ski resort**, if one considers that it looks down over the Golan Heights to the Sea of Galilee. For experienced skiers it is only really worth a visit for its novelty value. You can ski from December to April (depending on the snow) from the Moshav Neve Ativ village. Equipment can be hired at the resort and there are runs for all standards of skier but the snow is invariably slushy. Open 08:00–16:00 (http://hermonski.co.il).

▼ Below: Stark and dramatic scenery in the beautiful but disputed Golan Heights.

GALILEE AT A GLANCE

Best Times to Visit
The Sea of Galilee is below sea level and, though not as low as the Dead Sea, it does get very humid in summer. This does not, however, deter Israelis from flocking to its shores and beaches. **Spring** is a lovely time of year to visit, when the hills are green and the wild flowers are out. **Autumn**, from the end of September onwards, is more tolerable for hiking in the Golan Heights and for riding holidays. Winter is cooler and more temperate and there is skiing on Mount Hermon for a very limited season.

Getting There
Israel is small and Galilee is easily accessible by **road** from Jerusalem, Tel Aviv and Haifa. There are no trains or international airports here but Egged **buses** run between all the towns, with a central enquiry number, tel: 03 694 8888, www.egged. co.il Domestic flights operate to the airport at Rosh Pina, tel: 04 693 6478.

Getting Around
Several **car hire** companies have offices in Tiberias and Nazareth. Alternatively, **mountain bikes** are available from several of the hostels in and around Tiberias. A road runs right round the lake and there are plenty of trails in the hills and alongside the Hula Valley. **Taxis** and *sherut*

are available in Tiberias, Nazareth and Safed, where a private service operates, tel: 06 697 0707. Alternatively, take the Kinneret Sailing Company **ferry** from Kibbutz Ein Gev to Tiberias.

Where to Stay
The most luxurious hotels in this area are in **Tiberias**, a bustling resort. If you'd like to experience something different, try one of the kibbutz hotels which are reasonable, quite luxurious in some cases and a good introduction to kibbutz life.

TIBERIAS
Luxury
Leonardo Plaza Hotel, 1 Habanim Street, tel: 04 671 3333, www.leonardo-hotels. com Centrally located overlooking lake, full range of facilities including spa.
Gai Beach, Derech Hamerchatzaot Street, Tiberias, tel: 04 670 0700, www.gaibeachhotel.com Listed as 'luxury' but rooms a bit outdated. Popular among groups and families, fun waterpark.
Holiday Inn, Merhazaot Road, Tiberias, tel: 04 672 8555. Spa resort including the Tiberias hot springs. Horse-riding, tennis and beach facilities are all within walking distance.
Caesar Premier Hotel, Promenade 103, Gedud Barak Street, tel: 04 672

7272, www.caesarhotels.co.il/ en/ Modern hotel on promenade, heated mineral pool, gym and spa.

Mid-range
Hotel Eden, 4 Ohel Ya'akov Street, Tiberias, tel: 04 679 0070, www.edenhotel.co.il Quiet, modern hotel in the town centre, walking distance from the beach. Many activities on offer.
Kibbutz Maagan, Jordan Valley, tel: 04 665 4400, www.maagan.com Peaceful kibbutz-run holiday village on lake shore.
Ron Beach Hotel, Gedud Barak Street, Tiberias, tel: 04 679 1350, www.ronbeachhotel.com Low-rise beach hotel north of Tiberias with café, restaurant, pool and bar.

Budget
Poriya Guest House, Tiberias, tel: 02 594 5722, www.iyha.org.il Wooden cabins in garden setting near Poriya mountain south of Tiberias.

OUTSIDE TIBERIAS
Mid-range
Vered Hagalil Guest Farm, Korazim Junction, Jordan Valley, tel: 04 693 5785, www.veredhagalil.com A delightful ranch in a beautiful setting overlooking the lake. Western-style riding lessons and rides out, including overnight horseback safaris.

UPPER GALILEE
Mid-range
Kfar Giladi Kibbutz Hotel,
Upper Galilee, tel: 04 690
0000, www.kibbutz.cu.il
Beautiful views. Good facilities, including a large pool,
gym and a spa.

Budget
**Hagoshrim Kibbutz Resort
Hotel**, Upper Galilee,
tel: 04 681 6000,
www.hagoshrim-hotel.co.il
Kibbutz hotel with views of
Mount Hermon and the Golan
Heights.

WHERE TO EAT
Tiberias is packed with restaurants, their cuisine
ranging from South American
to Italian. Open-air fish restaurants line the lake shore;
don't miss the St Peter fish,
which is caught in the lake
and is very tasty. There are
rustic restaurants on the
kibbutzim out of town too.

Luxury
Pagoda, Gedud Barak Street,
Tiberias lake shore, tel: 04 672
5513. Superb Thai/Chinese
restaurant with outdoor seating overlooking the lake. Very
popular. Owners also operate
lake dinner cruises, some
with dancing.

Mid-range
Vered Hagalil (*see* Where
to Stay). Steak and local specialities in rustic setting with
views of the lake.

El Rancho Steak House,
1 Hakishon St, Tiberias,
tel: 053 809 4609. Popular
chain of kosher steak houses
nationwide.
Decks Charcoal Grill, Gedud
Barak Street, Tiberias, tel: 04
672 1538. Romantic dining
right on the waterfront –
grills and steaks. Kosher.

SHOPPING
The best shopping is in
Tiberias, which is good for
clothes, shoes and souvenirs, including special plastic
bottles that you can fill with
Jordan River water.
At the **Golan Heights Winery**
in Katzrin, there are tours
and tastings, tel: 04 696
8435, www.golanwines.co.il
For the best art galleries,
spend some time browsing
in Safed.

TOURS AND EXCURSIONS
Galilee is an adventure-
lover's paradise, with riding,
rafting, kayaking, abseiling,
gliding and 4WD adventures
all on offer. The **Jordan River
Park** north of the lake is great
for families and has picnic
areas, gentle kayaking and
inner tubing down the river.
In winter there's skiing on
Mount Hermon and in spring
and autumn, bird-watching
in the Hula Valley.
Several companies arrange
4WD excursions, riding and
outdoor activities. Try **Bat
Ya'ar** for horse riding, tel: 04
692 1788. Also within easy

reach of Galilee is the vast
archaeological site of Beit
She'an, tel: 04 658 7189.
Nimrod's Fortress in the
Golan Heights, tel: 04 694
9277. Conventional coach
tours of the biblical sites are
run by **Egged**.
All-terrain tours are run by
Avrami Jeep Tours, tel: 04
693 2133.
Jordan River rafting (summer): Kibbutz Gadot, Upper
Galilee, tel: 04 900 7000.
Kayak hire from Kfar Blum
Kibbutz, tel: 04 690 3388.
Horse-riding: Western-style
lessons and hacks as well as
overnight camping safaris
on horseback; Vered Hagalil
Farm, tel: 04 693 5785.
Mount Hermon Ski Resort,
tel: 1 599 550 560,
http://hermonski.co.il
Low altitude skiing in winter;
hiking, tours of former war
zones and extreme
tobogganing in summer.
Yardenit Baptismal Site
on the Jordan River for personal ceremonies,
tel: 04 675 9111,
www.yardenit.com

USEFUL CONTACTS
Tiberias Tourist information,
in front of Leonardo Plaza
Hotel, tel: 04 672 5666.
Maayan HaGoshrin,
adventure activities in upper
Galilee, tel: 04 681 6034.
Car rental:
Avis, tel: 04 672 2766;
Eldan, tel: 04 672 2831.

6
Haifa

Clinging to the side of **Mount Carmel** and spreading out around the busy port below, Haifa is Israel's third-largest city. From the sea, the mountain provides a beautiful backdrop, thick with bottle-green pines and elegant cypresses, while the golden dome of Haifa's **Baha'i Shrine** gleams in the sunlight, and elegant homes and villas nestle between the trees. Haifa has always been a safe haven for passing ships and it had a thriving Jewish community in the 11th century. However, it only become commercially important when the Ottoman Turks built the Hijaz railway between Damascus and Medina in 1905. The British constructed the harbour in 1934 and Haifa began to expand as it attracted more heavy industry. Today it's a centre for oil, chemicals, manu-facturing and electronics, while Israel's premier Institute of Technology, HaTechnion, sprawls across the Carmel hills. Haifa residents are fond of saying that 'Jerusalem prays, Tel Aviv parties and Haifa works' and there is indeed a bustling, businesslike atmosphere.

For visitors there are long, white sandy beaches, shady parks and gardens, interesting museums, religious sites and much walking or scrambling up and down Haifa's legendary stair paths.

Out of town, there's the lush, green expanse of **Carmel Park**, several fascinating **Druze Villages** to explore, and the mag-nificent remains at **Akko**, one of the oldest cities in the world. Further to the south are the carefully preserved **Roman remains** at Caesarea, perhaps Israel's most beautiful archaeological site.

DON'T MISS

*** The Baha'i Shrine: explore this beautiful building with its spectacular gardens.
*** Akko: absorb its amazing Crusader heritage.
*** Caesarea: easy day trip, impressive Roman remains.
** Carmel Centre: visit this centre for its shopping, dining and sweeping views.
** Druze Villages: enjoy their handicraft shopping.
** The Thousand Step Paths: a scenic way to see the city on foot.

◄ *Opposite: The inspiring hillside gardens of the Baha'i Shrine.*

113

HAIFA

COLOUR-CODED STAIRS

Haifa has four 'Thousand Stair Paths' – and yes, each has over 1000 stairs. The colour-coded paths descend through leafy neighbourhoods, hidden alley-ways and perfumed markets. The four are: the **yellow** route to the German Colony; the **red** route through Wadi Nisnas, the Arab Quarter; the **blue** route to Paris Square in the Old City; and the **green** route, also to the Old City. All four are marked on the tourist board maps.

HAIFA

Haifa is divided into three distinct areas: the **port and industrial zone**; **Mount Carmel**, the main centre of culture and entertainment; and **Hadar Ha-Carmel**, the business and commercial centre.

Baha'i Shrine ★★★

Haifa is known for its religious tolerance and is a fitting loca-tion for the world headquarters of the Baha'i faith, which preaches the unity of all world religions and believes that Moses, Jesus, Buddha and Mohammed were all fundamen-tally bearers of the same message. The faith has some four million followers worldwide.

Baha'i was founded in Persia and its leader, a prophet

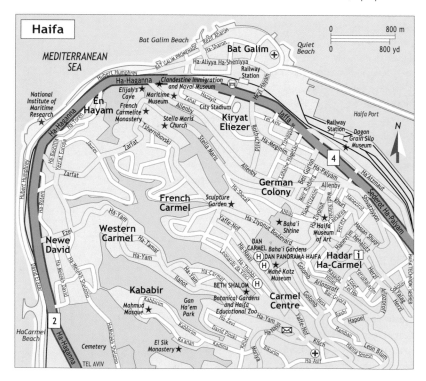

known as El Bab, was executed there for heretical preachings in 1850. His remains are kept in the Haifa mausoleum, now a centre of pilgrimage for Baha'i followers. Bab's successor, Mirza Hussein Ali, or Bahá'u'lláh, after whom the religion was named, is buried in the gardens in nearby **Akko**, the direction in which **Bab's shrine** on the hill faces.

The shrine itself, designated a UNESCO World Heritage Site in 2008, is magnificent, and the carefully manicured gardens a wonderfully shady place to rest. The gardens have since been extended to stretch from the mountain top to the seafront. Open 09:00–12:00 daily (inner gardens); 09:00–17:00 daily (outer gardens). Free tours in English daily at 12:00. No tours Wed.

▲ *Above: The shrine of the prophet El Bab is a centre of pilgrimage.*

Sculpture Garden ★

Further up the hillside along **Ha-Ziyonut Boulevard**, which twists its way across the mountain, is a beautiful sculpture garden containing more than 20 impressive bronze sculptures by Ursula Malbin. The garden has magnificent views of the coast, the northern mountains towards the Lebanese border and the bustling port below.

Haifa Educational Zoo ★

This research and education institution in Wadi Lotem on Mount Carmel, near Carmel Centre, displays more than 100 species without a single cage; all the animals are housed in open habitats, including bears and big cats. Other display spaces include waterfowl, vultures, lemurs and alligators. The zoo also has a Botanical Garden, home to dozens of tree and bush species from both the Carmel Mountain and Israel in general, and a Prehistoric Museum which covers the evolution of man in the Carmel region. Open 09:00–16:00 Sat–Thu; 09:00–14:00 Fri (winter).

Carmel Centre ★★★

Carmel Centre, on top of the mountain, is considered prime real estate with its shady trees and breathtaking views. Most of the big hotels and fashionable shops are along **Ha-Nassi**

BAB AND THE BAHA'I

Baha'i is one of the world's fastest-growing religions. The world's over five million followers live in some 120,000 locations in 236 countries and encompass over 2000 ethnic and tribal groups. Their belief is that there is only one God and that all the world's religions have been the various stages of his revelation to mankind. Baha'i principles include: the elimination of prejudice, equality between the sexes, the elimination of extremes of poverty and wealth, universal education, and the harmony of science and religion. Haifa's Shrine of the Bab, the faith's founder, is one of the holiest places in the Baha'i world.

HAIFA NIGHTLIFE

Haifa is a lively city and a thriving café society. Coffee shops all over the city serve delicious pastries and there are several bars and discos. Both the upmarket Panorama Mall and Carmel Centre have a string of good coffee shops (www.haifacity.com/eng/). Hasandak, located in the port area, is reckoned to be one of the best bars and Moriya Boulevard, south of Carmel Centre, is a happening club spot. There are also numerous performing arts venues and the Cinematek, which shows films in English.

Avenue, lined with restaurants and pavement cafés. From Derekh Ha-Yam Street, there's a short footpath, **Nahal Lotem**, which follows a *wadi* and has occasionally stunning views down over the city.

Stella Maris ★★

The mountain levels off into a north-facing promontory. At the top is the **French Carmelite Monastery**, established during the Third Crusade by a monastic and devout group of Crusaders. The monastery served as a hospital for Napoleon's troops during his unsuccessful siege of Akko against the Turks in 1799.

The nearby **Stella Maris Church** (1836), has beautiful, marble-covered walls and a gold dome adorned with biblical scenes, including one where the prophet, Elijah, is seen rising to Heaven. Its altar is situated directly over a small, rocky grotto which is believed by the Carmelites to have been the temporary home of Elijah. Open 08:00–12:30, 15:00–18:00 daily (times vary).

Elijah's Cave ★

Confusingly, there's another cave at the base of the cliff where Elijah is believed to have hidden on his flight from the evil King Ahab and his wife Jezebel. Furthermore, another legend states that the Holy Family took refuge in this cave on their return from Egypt, although the likelihood of the same cave being the site of two such important events hundreds of years apart (when there are plenty of other caves) is slim. Nonetheless Druze, Christians, Muslims and Jews all consider this a holy spot and pilgrims have left their mark on the stone walls. Open Sun–Thu 08:00–18:00; Fri 08:00–13:00 (summer).

Carmel by Cable Car ★★

Bubble-like cable cars, giving a recorded commentary on board, ferry visitors between **Stella Maris** and **Bat Galim**, the seafront

▼ *Below: Haifa has always been a safe haven for ships; in 1934 the British constructed the harbour which today serves the city's thriving industries.*

promenade. Needless to say, the views are splendid day and night, and the cable car is popular with locals in the evenings. Open daily 09:00–20:00 in summer, 10:00–18:00 in winter, closes earlier Fri (tel: 04 833 5970).

Naval Museum ★★

Near the bottom terminal of the cable car is a ship, the *Af-Al-Pi-Chen*, which means 'in spite of', commemorating the constant struggle to get illegal Jewish immigrants into Palestine under British rule, as Nazi fervour was stirred up in Europe during the 1930s and '40s. The *Af-Al-Pi-Chen* was one of the few ships that made it. The nearby Clandestine Immigration and Naval Museum shows some of the clever but often futile ways immigrants tried to enter the country. It has an atmosphere of struggle and despair similar to the Checkpoint Charlie Museum in Berlin. Open Sun–Thu 08:30–16:00.

▲ Above: Green Carmel Park provides a great escape from the bustle of the city.

Haifa Museum of Art ★

One of Israel's top three art galleries, the Haifa Museum of Art features an extensive exhibition of contemporary Israeli and international art on Shabbetai Levi Street in the Hadar district. It is in an historic building at the edge of Wadi Nisnas, itself a lynchpin for the three neighbourhoods – Jewish, Muslim and Christian – that meet at this site. Open 10:00–16:00 Sat–Wed; 10:00–19:00 Thu; 10:00–13:00 Fri.

Carmel Park ★★

Carmel Park, 8093ha (20,000 acres) of green space, hiking trails and picnic grounds, is the city's playground, peppered with pretty villages, caves, old settlements and magnificent views of the coast. The air is scented with pine, eucalyptus and cypress, and on a hot day the park is a great escape from the city.

PREHISTORIC MAN RECREATED

A good day out for all the family is a visit to the **Nahal Me'arot Caves** at Carmel, about 3km (2 miles) south of Ein Harod. The life of prehistoric man is recreated in a suitable cave setting through an audiovisual presentation and a film. Children can have a go at reconstructing the tools used by prehistoric man. Tours in English are available. Open 08:00–16:00 Sun–Thu (winter), 08:00–17:00 (summer), 08:00–15:00 Fri.

HAIFA

DRUZE VILLAGES

Isfiya and **Daliat al Carmel**, some 16km (10 miles) south-east of the Mount Carmel ridge, are two villages inhabited by the Druze religious sect. Daliat al Carmel has a great **handicraft market** every day except Friday (the Druze Shabbat) and makes an interesting stop for shopping and browsing for copperware and basketry.

AKKO

Jutting out into the northern end of the **Bay of Haifa**, Akko is known for its amazing 12th-century **fortified city** built by the Crusaders. Akko's domes, minarets and solid-looking walls have seen their share of action. First a Phoenician port, Akko fell to the Arabs in 636 and became an Arab colony. The Crusaders later made Akko their principal port, but in 1291 the Mamelukes took the town. In 1749 a Bedouin sheik set up his own independent fiefdom here and set about restoring the city. He built the White Market, installed access roads and rebuilt the port and city walls. In 1799, the pasha of Akko, Ahmed Al-Jazzar, added fortifications to the city after holding off Napoleon, whose dreams of an empire in the East thereafter dissolved. In 1917 Akko was captured by Britain, but with Israel's independence in 1948, it was taken over by the Jews.

Visitors can admire the sites, take a boat around the ancient harbour to see the dense walls, and wander through the noisy, narrow streets of the *souq*. Several fish restaurants have fine views across the harbour.

Mosque of Al-Jazzar ★★

Israel's third-largest mosque, the green-domed Al-Jazzar, was built in 1781 in the style of the Ottoman Turks and is encircled by arcades, covering a large part of the city built by the Crusaders 500 years previously. Visits by appointment; tel: 04 991 3039.

ARMED FOR ARMAGEDDON

The Book of Revelations states that the final battle of mankind, Armageddon, will take place on the plains around **Har Megiddo**, a town on the floor of the Jezreel Valley east of Haifa in the Galilee area.

▼ *Below: Caesarea's Roman amphitheatre is remarkably intact.*

Crusader City ★★★

Across the street from the mosque, the subterranean Crusader City is dark, damp and eerie. The vast Entrance Hall is adorned with 800-year-old frescoes, and leads to the cavernous **Crypt of St John**, where the knights would hide from attackers. This crypt was later adopted by Al-Jazzar as his own escape route should Napoleon break down his defences. Because of the danger of collapsing ceilings, only certain areas are open to visitors. Open 08:30–17:00 Sun–Thu (winter); 08:30–14:00 Fri.

Municipal Museum ★★

Located in an old Turkish bathhouse, the nearby museum gives a good grounding in local Crusader and Islamic history, with archaeological exhibits and ancient weapons.

▲▼ *Above and below: Surprising details, ancient and modern, at Caesarea.*

CAESAREA

This is one of Israel's most beautiful archaeological sites. Crumbling walls and tumbled pillars jut out into the water and some of the ruins are actually submerged. Caesarea was built in 22–10BC by **Herod** in his usual lavish style and dedicated to Augustus Caesar, emperor of the time. The city had a reputation for violence, and the massacre of 20,000 Jews here sparked off the first uprising against the Romans in AD66.

In the 4th century, Rome fell and a Christian community thrived in Caesarea, before Arab armies invaded in 639. Crusaders arrived in 1101 and made off with what they believed to be the Holy Grail. Muslims later pillaged the city and left it to rot, while sand dunes and water gradually covered its once-majestic buildings.

Excavations in the 1950s led to the restoration of some of the magnificent buildings. You can see the massive **aqueduct**, a stunning **Roman amphitheatre**, the **hippodrome** and a variety of Crusader remains, as well as the ten-minute Travel Through Time multimedia display that tells the story of the area's history. Open 09:00–18:00 Sat–Thu, 09:00–16:00 Fri (Apr–Sep); 09:00–16:00 Sat–Thu, 09:00–15:00 Fri (Oct–Mar).

ARTISTS' HAVEN

A short drive or bus journey to the south of Haifa is the charming artists' colony of **Ein Hod**, a village where every other house is an art gallery. Ein Hod was started in 1953 and is a pretty collection of Moorish-style houses set amongst olive trees. Wander round the narrow streets admiring the work or browse for prints in the many shops. At the village centre, the Janco-Dada Museum houses the more prestigious pieces. It is open 09:30–15:30 Sun–Thu, 09:30–14:00 Fri, 10:00–16:00 Sat.

HAIFA AT A GLANCE

BEST TIMES TO VISIT
Haifa is warm and sunny **all year round**, although the summer months of July, August and September can become very humid.

GETTING THERE
Ben Gurion International, Israel's main airport, is situated 20km (12½ miles) from Tel Aviv. Haifa is an hour's drive from here. There are direct **trains** from Ben Gurion, www.rail.co.il, call centre: 077 232 4000.
Haifa is also a major port with **passenger shipping services** to several European cities.

GETTING AROUND
Israel's only **subway** – the Carmelit – goes from the old city and port up to Central Carmel, tel: 04 837 6861, www.carmelithaifa.com
Part of **Egged's BRT** (bus rapid transport) system, the new electronic **Metronit** is extensive, tel: 03 639 4444, www.bus.co.il
For sightseers, a **cable car** goes up the mountainside. For the energetic, the tourist board has marked four colour-coded **walking trails**, the Thousand Steps Paths. Start at the top of the mountain and walk down, rather than the other way round.

WHERE TO STAY
Haifa has a good range of luxury hotels but gets very busy in July and August, when Baha'i pilgrims flood into the city. The best place for visitors to stay is Carmel Centre, which is close to the shops and has panoramic views of the city.

Luxury
Dan Carmel, 85–87 Ha-Nassi Avenue, Haifa, tel: 04 830 3030, www.danhotels.com
This five-star hotel near central Carmel is close to shopping, zoo and parks. It has a swimming pool and spa and fitness room.
Dan Panorama Haifa, 107 Ha-Nassi Avenue, Haifa, tel: 04 835 2222. Located in central Carmel with dizzying views of the city below. Huge gym; Panorama Mall and Carmel Centre nearby.
Dan Caesarea Hotel, Caesarea, tel: 04 626 9111. Resort hotel on the coast, near Caesarea harbour and Israel's only golf course (18 holes).

Mid-range
Beit Oren Hotel, Kibbutz Beit Oren, Carmel National Park, Haifa, tel: 04 830 7444. Kibbutz hotel on Mount Carmel, some 17km (10 miles) from Haifa. Holistic treatments, swimming pool and horse-riding available.
Beth Shalom Hotel, 101 HaNassi Avenue, Haifa, tel: 04 837 7481, www.beth-shalom.co.il
Small, simple and basic, but comfortable three-star in central Carmel, near shops and nightlife.
Carmel Forest Spa Resort, tel: 04 830 7888, www.isrotelexclusivecollection.com Part of the Isrotel hotel chain. Health and beauty packages offered.
Shulamit Hotel, 15 Kiryat Sefer Street, Haifa, tel: 04 834 2811, www.hotels-of-israel.com. Four-star hotel on Mount Carmel surrounded by pine gardens.

Budget
Dan Gardens, 124 Yaffe-Nof Street, Haifa, tel: 04 830 2020. Part of Dan Hotels, compact, affordable bed and breakfast on Mount Carmel.

WHERE TO EAT
Haifa has a great choice of restaurants and a lively nightlife. You can wander through Wadi Nisnas, the Arab Quarter, in the early evening and soak up the atmosphere. Crowds of office workers visit the falafel cafés on their way home for a snack and the air is thick with delicious aromas and the sights and sounds of the *souqs*. **Hazkenim** and **Michel**, falafel shops on opposite sides of the main road, vie for the title of the best falafel establishment in Israel.
Nightlife tends to be aimed

at the locals and there are several bars with music in addition to nightclubs. The 24-hour 'What's on in Haifa' website is the best source of information (see Useful Contacts below). Worth a visit is the entertainment complex at the modern, hi-tech convention centre on the seafront, with a multiscreen cinema, some designer shops and a couple of theme restaurants.

Luxury
Dolphin, 13 Bat Gallm Avenue, Haifa, tel: 04 852 3837/7149. Smart seafood restaurant.
Rak Basar, 15 Ben Gurion Boulevard, tel: 04 855 1872. Housed in a beautifully restored mansion in the German Colony, rak basar means 'meat only'.

Mid-range
Jacko's, 12 Kehilat Saloniki Street (downtown Haifa), tel: 04 866 8813. Unpretentious, noisy, shared tables, excellent fish and seafood dishes.

Budget
Abu Yusef, 1 Ha-Maginim Street, off Paris Square, tel: 04 866 3723. Excellent no-frills Lebanese food.
Klein's Cafe, 96 HaNassi Boulevard, tel: 057 944 0985. Third-floor panoramic views over Baha'i Gardens.

SHOPPING
Judaica in every shape or form is on sale in Haifa and the places you'll visit on tours. Cookbooks, history books, menorahs (seven-branched candlesticks), seder plates (for Passover), matza covers, educational children's toys, jewellery, and kipas (skull caps) in everything from satin to suede are available. Loose diamonds are also good value.
For a good mall, try the **Castra Art, Recreation and Shopping Centre** at 8 Moshe Fliman Street. It's a huge, modern complex of galleries, shops and restaurants with a busy cultural programme of exhibitions, tel: 04 859 0001.

TOURS AND EXCURSIONS
Tour Operators in Haifa
The tourist office (www.visit-haifa.org/eng/) offers city tours, walking tours, downtown tours and religious tours, tel: 04 853 5606. All tour operators feature trips to Jerusalem, Tel Aviv, Akko, Caesarea and further afield.
Egged Tours (tel: 03 920 3992, www.eggedtours.com) offers tours all over the country.
Israel My Way, 22 HaAshlag Street, tel: 077 300 5717.
Society for the Protection of Nature in Israel (nature trails), 90 Yafo Street, Haifa, tel: 04 855 3860, http://natureisrael.org/haifa

USEFUL CONTACTS
Car Rental
Avis, tel: 04 867 2111.
Taxi & Sherut Hire
tel: 04 866 4444/6.
Amal Taxi, tel: 04 866 2324.
Regular Taxi
Moriah, tel: 04 826 1271.
Carmiel, tel: 04 852 3882.
Bus Information
Egged runs the Metronit, and urban and inter-urban bus lines. For Egged Haifa, tel: 03 914 5818, www.egged.co.il; for Metronit, tel: *8787 (within Israel). There are two Central Bus Stations in Haifa: Merkazit Hof ha-Karmel and 1 Zore'a Me'ir St.
Carmelit Subway Information
The Carmelit subway system travels between six stations. It is a 24hr service, with shorter hours on Fri and Sat, tel: 04 837 6861/2231, www.carmelithaifa.com
Train Information,
tel: *5770, www.rail.co.il/EN/

Tourist Information
Haifa Tourist Association (German Colony), 48 Ben Gurion Avenue, tel: 04 853 5606, www.visit-haifa.org/eng/

What's on in Haifa
www.haifacity.com/eng/

Travel Tips

TOURIST INFORMATION

There are Israel Government Tourist Offices in 14 locations around the world including the UK, the USA and Canada. In Israel, most major towns and cities have an information office and there are several in both Jerusalem and Tel Aviv. These include: Ben Gurion Airport Entrance Hall. tel: 03 975 4260, open 24/7; Tel Aviv Tourism Association, Clocktower, Jaffa, open Sun–Thu 09:00–17:30, Fri 09:30–14:00; Tel Aviv Tourism Association, Tel Aviv Promenade, 46 Herbert Samuel St, tel: 03 516 6188, open Sun–Thu 09:30–17:30, Fri 09:00–13:00; Jerusalem Tourist Information, Jaffa Gate, Omar Ibn Katab Square in the Old City, tel: 02 628 0403, open Sat–Thu 08:30–17:00, Fri 08:30–13:00. Other major towns also have a **Tourist Information Office**: Eilat: 8 Beit Hagesher Street, tel: 08 630 9111; Haifa: 48 Ben Gurion Boulevard, tel. 04 853 5606; Tiberias: Ha-Banim Street, The Archaeological Park, tel: 06 672 5666. Also try www.goisrael.com or www.thinkisrael.com

ENTRY REQUIREMENTS

Travellers to Israel need a valid passport. Check with the Israeli Embassy whether a visa is required. Citizens of most countries, including Australia, Canada, South Africa, the UK and the USA are issued a visa on entry. The normal permitted length of stay is three months, although if you are a cruise passenger just visiting for the day, you will simply receive a landing card. On entering Israel, expect to be questioned at length, particularly if you have Arabic stamps in your passport. This can seem intimidating and the best is to be polite and to offer straight answers. The same will happen when you leave Israel; you will be questioned about what's in your luggage before you check it in and it will probably be X-rayed before you even join the check-in queue. Israel has a limited number of entry points. The three international airports are Tel Aviv's Ben Gurion, Eilat's Ovda and Haifa. Cruise passengers arrive at Haifa or Ashdod, while there are several points of entry by road (see Getting There, page 123). If you plan to visit countries which may deny you entry if you have an Israeli stamp in your passport, you can ask for the stamp to be placed on a separate piece of paper, but this is offered less readily than in the past. You'll also have problems entering the West Bank if your passport is not stamped.

VISITING THE WEST BANK

Most tourists visit the West Bank in order to see Bethlehem as a day trip from Jerusalem, or to transit the area en route to the Dead Sea spa resorts, the Negev and the South. Travel within the West Bank is not possible without passing through multiple Israeli military checkpoints. These checkpoints are flash points for violent incidents and have been the scene of several fatal attacks, so be vigilant. Even on a day trip, take ID with you and prepare for delays. For more in-depth travel, you must consult the Israel Ministry of Foreign Affairs (www.mfa.gov.il) or, for example, the British Foreign Office (www.gov.uk) or the US Dept of State (www.state.goc/travel/).

CUSTOMS

The following items do not need to be declared. Any other items must be declared in the Red Channel at entry points. **Spirits**, up to one litre, plus two litres of wine per person over 17. **Perfumes**, up to 1/4 litre per person. **Tobacco**, up to 250g or 250 cigarettes per person over 17. **Gifts** (excluding the above) up to $200 per person. **Camcorders**, **personal computers** and **diving equipment** must be declared and a refundable deposit paid. On

exit, tourists can claim VAT refunds for items bought from shops bearing the 'tax VAT refund' logo. Antiques (anything made before 1700) may not be exported without a written approval from the Antiquities Authority, www.antiquities.org.il

HEALTH REQUIREMENTS
No vaccinations are required to enter Israel except yellow fever if arriving from an infected area.

GETTING THERE
Points of entry
Most people enter at Ben Gurion International Airport outside Tel Aviv. There are land crossings on the borders with Jordan and Egypt.

By air
Airlines from all over the world fly to Ben Gurion International Airport, including the national carrier, **El Al** (tel: 03 977 1111, www.elal.co.il). More and more airlines are starting services to Israel as tourism grows. Travellers from the UK can now choose between **Easyjet** (www.easyjet.com), **Iberia** (www.iberia.com), and **British Airways** (www.ba.com). From the USA, there are nonstop flights from Atlanta, Los Angeles, Miami and both New York's JFK and Newark-Liberty airports. **Air Canada** (www.aircanada.com) flies nonstop from Toronto and Montreal to Tel Aviv. Flight time from New York to Tel Aviv is ten hours. Domestic flights within Israel are operated by **Arkia**

Airlines (tel. 03 690 2210, www.arkia.com). Arkia flies between Tel Aviv (Ben Gurion or Sde Dov) and Haifa and Eilat, as well as operating low-cost flights to European destinations. **Israir** also flies between Sde Dov and Eilat, as well as operating low-cost flights to a few European cities; tel. 03 510 9589, www.israirairlines.com
Israel Airport Authority, tel: 03 975 5555; online flight arrivals and departures in English: www.iaa.gov.il/Rashat/en-US/Airports/BenGurion/

By boat
A few cruise lines dock at **Haifa** and **Ashdod** and there is a ferry service from here to Cyprus. Passengers can board in Cyprus, Greece, Turkey or Egypt and enter Israel through Haifa Port, Tel Aviv, Ashdod or Eilat. Israel has many marinas with facilities for private yachts (www.goisrael.com).

By road
Land entry into Israel is possible through Egypt and Jordan. Border crossings are under the jurisdiction of the Israel Airports Authority. There are three points of entry from Jordan: the **Yitzhak Rabin Border Terminal** at Eilat, tel: 08 630 0555; the **Allenby Border Terminal** east of Jericho and an hour's drive from Jerusalem, tel: 02 548 2600; and the **Jordan River Border Terminal** at Beit She'an, tel: 04 609 3400. There are two crossings

from Egypt, the **Taba Border Terminal** at Eilat, tel: 08 636 0999, and **Nitzana**, tel:08 656 4666. The type of traffic allowed through these crossings varies according to the security situation, as do the opening times, so check the Israel Airports Authority website:www.iaa.gov.il/Rashat/en-US/Rashot/FAQ/

WHAT TO PACK
Even for business, Israelis are fairly casual. Remember to bring sunglasses, sunscreen and a hat; swimming gear; walking shoes; and long sleeves and long trousers or a long skirt for entering religious sites. In winter, bring rainwear and sweaters.

MONEY MATTERS
The unit of currency is the **New Israeli shekel** (NIS), divided into 100 **agorot**. You can bring an unlimited amount of cash or traveller's cheques into the country. Some shops accept foreign currency, although change will be in shekels. Most credit cards are acceptable. Some banks have automatic teller machines. Money can also be exchanged at hotels. VAT in Israel is currently 18%, except in Eilat, which is a duty-free zone for tourists. Note: The duty-free shops at Ben Gurion International Airport only take **dollars**.
Banking hours: These vary, but generally 08:30–12:00 Sunz-Fri, 16:00–18:00 Sun, Tue, Thu. Some branches close Fri or Sun.

TRAVEL TIPS

ACCOMMODATION

Hotels range from simple hostels to luxury establishments, graded from two to five stars. Rates are quoted in US dollars and do not include a 15% service charge. Although **kibbutz** communal life is declining in the strictly traditional sense, there are plenty of hotels in the Kibbutz Hotels Chain, making up the country's largest hotel group. Book each hotel individually through the website www.kibbutz.co.il There's one kibbutz hotel in Tel Aviv and several around Jerusalem, though not in the city centre. There are **youth hostels** all over Israel, listed on www.iyha.org.il (tel: 1 599 510 511), including two in Jerusalem, one in Tel Aviv and one in Jaffa. The country also has a wide network of **Christian guesthouses**, offering more modest accommodation aimed at practising Christians. There's a list on www.travelujah.com Alternatively, visitors can book a bed-and-breakfast property in Jerusalem direct with the owner via www.bnb.co.il and in Tel Aviv via www.airbnb.com/s/Tel-Aviv--Israel which features B&B accommodation which features different types of B&B accommodation.

EATING OUT

Cuisine from all over the world is available in Israel. Kosher restaurants – which could be anything from Israeli dishes to Chinese or international cuisine – are to be found in all hotels and in many towns. These avoid mixing meat and dairy products, so a restaurant will either serve meat dishes or vegetarian and dairy. Pork is not served in Jewish, kosher or Muslim restaurants, and seafood is not sold in kosher establishments. Oriental restaurants in Israel serve Middle Eastern food, not Asian as the name might imply. This is great for vegetarians and meat eaters alike, with a huge range of *meze* (snack) dishes on offer. Travellers on a budget can do very well at the ubiquitous falafel stalls in every town, where pitta bread is packed with falafel balls and salad. Water from the tap is drinkable in Israel but if you prefer bottled water, it is also sold everywhere.

TRANSPORT

Air
Domestic flights within Israel are operated by **Arkia Airlines** and **Israir** (*see* Getting There, page 123).

Road
Israel has an excellent road network and most major **car hire** firms operate here. Drivers require an international licence or a licence written in English or French. You'll also need to be over 21 and hold an international credit card to rent a car. There are plenty of repair garages and petrol stations. Petrol is cheaper than in Europe but car rental can be expensive. Parking is difficult in towns; a kerb marked with blue and white means you need a parking ticket, bought in blocks from kiosks and tobacconists. Fines and clamping are strictly enforced. **Taxis** are metered and may be hailed on the streets. A *sherut* is a shared taxi, with a fixed price per passenger.

Buses
The bus network is excellent and reasonably priced. Most urban and inter-urban bus services are operated by the vast **Egged Bus Cooperative**, tel: 03 694 8888, www.egged.co.il Local and intercity transport in Tel Aviv and the surrounding suburbs is also provided by **Dan** bus company (tel: 03 639 4444, www.dan.co.il) or try www.bus.co.il

CONVERSION CHART		
From	**To**	**Multiply By**
Millimetres	Inches	0.0394
Metres	Yards	1.0936
Metres	Feet	3.281
Kilometres	Miles	0.6214
Square kilometres	Square miles	0.386
Hectares	Acres	2.471
Litres	Pints	1.760
Kilograms	Pounds	2.205
Tonnes	Tons	0.984

To convert Celsius to Fahrenheit: x 9 ÷ 5 + 32

Timetables are available from tourist information offices and bus stations. To travel from Jerusalem and Tel Aviv to Eilat, you may need to book in advance. Buses do not run from sundown on Friday to sundown on Saturday and on Jewish holidays.

Trains
Israel Railways Corporation has eight routes including a fast connection from Tel Aviv to Jerusalem. Fares are comparable to buses, and seats can be booked in advance. Trains usually have a buffet car. Like buses, trains do not run on Shabbat or holidays. For information, tel. 077 232 4000, www.rail.co.il

Hitchhiking
Although Israel was historically a fine place in which to hitchhike, the practice is increasingly dangerous now and is not recommended.

BUSINESS HOURS
Business and shopping hours are usually from 09:00–19:00 Sun–Thu, some closing between 14:00 and 16:00. On Fridays and holidays, shops close at midday. Some stores close Tue afternoon.

TIME DIFFERENCE
Depending on daylight saving, Israel is two hours ahead of Greenwich Mean Time and seven hours ahead of Eastern Standard Time.

COMMUNICATIONS
Israelis are avid newspaper readers and there are several dozen dailies, most with a po-

litical leaning. *The Jerusalem Post* and *Ha'aretz* are published Sun–Fri in English, while the *Jerusalem Report* is a bi-weekly magazine in English. There are daily and weekly publications in Arabic, French, Spanish and Russian.

TV AND RADIO
In early 2014 the **Israel Broadcasting Authority**, whose main commercial networks consisted of Channel 2 and Channel 10 news operations, began massive infrastructural changes that will see it closed down and replaced by a brand-new broadcasting body. Most households, however, subscribe to cable or satellite TV. This includes **BBC World Service**, **CNN** and **Sky**, as well as **Lebanese** and **Jordanian** English channels. Numerous commercial radio stations carry everything from pop music to ultra-Orthodox programming.

POST
Hours are 07:00–21:00 Sun–Thu, 07:00–14:00 Fri. Postboxes are red for out of town and international, yellow for local post.

TELEPHONE
The country code for Israel is +972. Israeli area codes commence with a zero, e.g. 02 123 4567, so if you are calling Israel from overseas, drop the zero (e.g. +972 2 123 4567). Israelis have more cellphones per capita than any nationality on earth. Even children have them. If your cell phone and/

ROAD SIGNS

Road signs in Israel appear in English, Hebrew and Arabic. Driving is on the right. Israelis use their horns a lot and tend to drive aggressively in cities, but rural roads are not congested. Seat belts must be worn at all times and children under four strapped into child car seats. Speed limits are 120km/h (75mph) on major highways; 80km/h (30–50mph) in urban areas. A blue-and-white painted kerb means you need a parking token, which you can buy in a machine, at a kiosk or from some shops. Red-and-white kerbs mean no parking. The penalty is a fine, a clamp or being towed away.

or handheld wireless device is programmed for international service, it will work automatically in Israel, though roaming charges can be high. Alternatively, cell phones can be rented as you arrive in Israel, or you can buy an Israeli SIM card at Ben Gurion airport. There are public phones throughout Israel. You'll need to buy a Telecart magnetic card to use them. These are available at newsstands, supermarkets, post offices or at your hotel front desk. Most hotels and many public places have Wi-Fi internet at reasonable prices. For area codes, *see* panel, page 57.

ELECTRICITY
Electric current is 220v AC, single phase, 50 Hertz. Plugs are three-pronged round pin; you'll need an adaptor.

TRAVEL TIPS

- **Holy Bible** – only in Israel does the Bible come so comprehensively to life.
- Winter, Dick, **Culture Shock – Israel** (1992) Kuperard, London: Insiders' guide to politics, religion and life in Israel.
- Schiff, Z and Yaari, E, **Israel's Lebanon War** (1984) Simon and Schuster, New York.
- Schiff, Z and Yaari, E, **Intifada** (1990) Simon and Schuster, New York: Modern history recounted by two of Israel's best-known journalists.
- Bar-Zohar, Michael, **Ben-Gurion** (1978) Delacorte, New York: official biography of the founder of Israel.

WEIGHTS AND MEASURES

Israel uses the metric system.

HEALTH PRECAUTIONS

The biggest health risk to tourists is sunstroke, sunburn, and, consequently, dehydration. Respect the sun in Israel; it is most dangerous between 10:00 and 16:00.

HEALTH SERVICES

Israel has an excellent medical system but visitors should always have private medical insurance as costs can be high. Doctors will come to hotel rooms or can be visited at an emergency room at a **Magen David Adom** (similar to the Red Cross) hospital. For an ambulance, dial 101. **Pharmacists** operate on a rota basis, the schedule for which is published in the *Jerusalem Post*. Many speak English. You will need a prescription for stronger drugs.

PERSONAL SAFETY

Petty crime – theft, mugging and car crime – is common but violent crime much less so. Visitors can feel very secure wandering around the cities at night. But don't flash wealth around ostentatiously and don't leave anything valuable in a car or hotel room. **Security** is the biggest issue; report any suspicious packages and never leave bags lying around because they may be blown up. Before travelling to the West Bank, be sure to check a trusted travel advisory about the security situation.

EMERGENCIES

Police, tel: 100.
Ambulance, tel: 101.
Fire Brigade, tel: 102.
There's a special tourist police division of the police force which deals with everyday matters affecting travellers.

ETIQUETTE

Tipping in restaurants is usually 10–15%. Taxi drivers appreciate but do not expect a tip, while *sherut* drivers need not be tipped. Conservative dress is essential for visiting religious sites. Men should wear a *kippa*, or skullcap; in many places, like the Western Wall on Shabbat, one is provided. Shoes should be removed when entering a mosque. Topless sunbathing is frowned upon. Israelis are generally very direct and open and may strike up a conversation with a stranger in any public place or restaurant. Learn to embrace this attitude rather than shy away from it; the questions may seem personal but this is the Israeli culture! Respect the Sabbath. Everything starts to wind down on a Friday afternoon and in Jerusalem in particular, will grind to a complete stop. In a kosher hotel restaurant, the breakfast coffee and bread on a Saturday will have been made the day before (so for a decent Saturday breakfast, find a non-kosher place). Don't ask observant Jews to do anything like attend a business meeting on a Friday afternoon. Do not expect to get anything done on a Jewish holiday (even El Al doesn't fly). When checking in for an El Al flight or crossing borders, do not be offended by rigorous and repeated questioning; it's nothing personal.

LANGUAGE

Hebrew is the official language, along with **Arabic**. **English** is learned as a second language in schools. French, Spanish, German, Yiddish, Russian, Polish and Hungarian are widely spoken. Road signs appear in Hebrew, Arabic and English.

PUBLIC HOLIDAYS AND FESTIVALS

The official holidays are Jewish holidays and *Shabbat*, but each religion has the right to observe its own holidays, of which there are many. Public holidays and *Shabbat* take place from sunset to sunset. The main ones are listed in the panel on page 24.

INDEX

INDEX